FINDING
MIDAS

FINDING MIDAS

INVESTING IN ENTREPRENEURIAL CEOs
WITH THE GOLDEN TOUCH

PRESIDENT AND CEO OF RENN CAPITAL GROUP

RUSSELL CLEVELAND

with Bette Price

Published by Greenleaf Book Group Press
4425 S. Mo Pac Expy., Suite 600, Austin, TX 78735

Distributed by Greenleaf Book Group LP

For ordering information or special discounts for bulk purchases, please contact Greenleaf Book Group LP at 4425 S. Mo Pac Expy., Suite 600, Austin, TX 78735 (512) 891-6100.

Design and composition by Greenleaf Book Group LP
Cover design by Greenleaf Book Group LP

Publisher's Cataloging-In-Publication Data:
(Prepared by The Donohue Group, Inc.)

Cleveland, Russell.
  Finding Midas : investing in entrepreneurial CEOs with the golden touch / Russell Cleveland, with Bette Price. -- 1st ed.

  p. ; cm.

  ISBN-13: 978-1-929774-43-2
  ISBN-10: 1-929774-43-5

1. Investments--United States. 2. Investment analysis--United States. 3. Chief executive officers. 4. Leadership. I. Price, Bette. II. Title.

HG4529 .C54 2007
338.7   2007922309

Printed in the United States of America on acid-free paper

07 08 09 10 11 12   10 9 8 7 6 5 4 3 2 1

First Edition

To the Entrepreneurs of the world.
Thank you for creating jobs and economic growth.

"Simplicity is the ultimate sophistication."
— LEONARDO DA VINCI

CONTENTS

PREFACE

THE ENTREPRENEURIAL CEO INVESTING concept I introduce in this book is the result of my nearly fifty years of investment experience. I began my career in 1961 after graduating from the Wharton School of Business, University of Pennsylvania, when I joined the old-line investment banking firm of Kidder, Peabody and Company. Since then I have been directly involved in the investing process, devoting the majority of my time to managing private partnerships and a number of closed-end mutual funds. In 1973 I became the principal founder and majority shareholder of RENN Capital Group, Inc., which is the investment manager of the funds.

My experience has been concentrated in emerging growth companies whose capitalization is under $300 million but whose principal is in the $10-to-$100-million range. In this arena I have achieved a noteworthy track record. Lipper ranked Renaissance Capital Growth & Income Fund III, Inc., the number one closed-end fund among its peer group in net asset value growth for 2004 and one-, three-, five-, and ten-year periods through 2006.

Renaissance U.S. Growth Investment Trust PLC was ranked number one for one-, three-, and five-year periods among U.S. smaller company trusts traded in Great Britain.

In recent decades I have focused more on active investment management, serving on boards of directors of companies to help them grow directly, as opposed to merely buying shares in the stock market. These combined experiences have given me some unusual insights into what works and what doesn't as it relates to business investments. For example, at the beginning of 2007, my Renaissance U.S. Growth Investment Trust PLC fund was up 360 percent from its inception ten years ago, and U.S. holdings of the U.S. Special Opportunities Trust PLC, traded on the London Stock Exchange, have advanced 200 percent since 2001. This approach to growth continues to prove itself.

A portion of the genesis of my Entrepreneurial CEO Investing idea actually began some years ago when I was writing an investment column for *Texas Business* magazine. I titled one article "CEO Investing" based on a conversation I'd had with a gentleman named Richard Henshen, a very successful venture capitalist. Henshen began his venture capital work as a hands-on type of investor after leaving Texas Instruments. He got involved in the technology, sales, and marketing of various aspects of companies. In the process, he learned that his micromanaging approach was not nearly as successful as when he concentrated all his attention on selecting and working with the company's CEO.

Henshen had a unique philosophy. He believed that if the CEO had a personal investment in the company, he was much more likely to succeed. He could make money not only for himself but also for the other investors. If he failed, he would be as financially hurt as any of the investors. As a result, the risk and reward were balanced.*

I was intrigued with Henshen's approach and began to examine CEOs in a new light. I began to view them not only from a management standpoint but also according to their successful leadership characteristics, their philosophies, and their commitments to ownership as these characteristics related to their position in the stock market. As you will see, this book contains many examples that illustrate this underlying principle: If you follow a specific set of criteria in selecting the right CEO in whom to invest, follow that CEO's strategies and actions for a number of years, and, accordingly, stay with the investment, your returns could be quite exceptional. For example, a $10,000 investment in Bill Gates when he first took Microsoft public would be valued in excess of $4,250,000 in the year 2007. This return far outstrips such indexes as the Standard & Poor's 500 or the Dow Jones Industrial Average.

An integral part of the Entrepreneurial CEO Investing techniques I have been refining in my own investment experience was developed with the help of my longtime friend and colleague Richard Tozer, Ph.D. A former professor of finance

---

* For simplicity of style and ease of reading, I will use the masculine pronoun when referring to CEOs throughout the book. I am not trying to ignore female CEOs, who have emerged in recent years, but because the majority are men, I have opted for this pronoun choice.

at Southern Methodist University, Dr. Tozer has been a successful management consultant for many years. He and I formulated a number of checklists and tools that I use for determining which of the many opportunities are best for investment. Together with professor Jerry White, Dr. Tozer and I have conducted numerous seminars for the graduate program at SMU, concentrating on entrepreneurial leadership. We continue to refine the concept of Entrepreneurial CEO Investing and are now ready to expand the awareness of just how important this concept is to the investment experience.

Along the way I encountered another colleague, Bette Price, whose research for and authorship of the book *True Leaders* support our checklist of critical CEO characteristics. I invited her to join my efforts to make *Finding Midas* as helpful as possible to you, the reader-investor, so that you too can embrace this simple, dramatically successful investment system.

I have always said my epitaph should read "Russell Cleveland—Lifetime Student." In the investment area we are all students, learning, growing, and hopefully not making the same mistakes twice.

RUSSELL CLEVELAND
President, RENN Capital Group, Inc.

INTRODUCTION

WOULDN'T IT BE GREAT to wake up each morning knowing that you're vested in a viable, safe and sound, realistic investment strategy that will allow you to sleep well at night and to enter your retirement years able to live a very comfortable lifestyle? Start reading now because that is exactly what is in store for you. Entrepreneurial CEO Investing is at the heart of a system we call "finding the mega-stocks," that is, stocks that appreciate to 10-20-100-1,000 times your investment. If you are patient, a small investment could turn into a sizable fortune, as illustrated by the examples we include of Entrepreneurial CEO Investing and the mega-gains that occurred in each case.

We have also selected ten entrepreneurs across ten industries, all of whom would meet the criteria described in this book. Part II of *Finding Midas* contains a case study of each of the CEOs, and the book's conclusion includes an investment grid and the companies' annual growth rates. You will probably agree, the numbers are staggering and beat all the various stock indexes by miles.

$10,000 INVESTMENT			
CEO Name	Company & Symbol	Year Company Went Public	Current Value*
Warren Buffett	Berkshire Hathaway (NYSE: BRK/A)	1965	$54,425,000
Michael Dell	Dell (NASDAQ: DELL)	1988	$2,917,000
Bill Gates	Microsoft (NASDAQ: MSFT)	1986	$4,257,000
J. R. Hyde III	AutoZone (NYSE: AZO)	1991	$207,000
Herb Kelleher	Southwest Airlines (NYSE: LUV)	1971	$1,600,000
Lowry Mays	Clear Channel (NYSE: CCU)	1981	$1,175,000
Angelo Mozilo	Countrywide Financial Corp. (NYSE: CFC)	1969	$3,000,000
Howard Schultz	Starbucks (NASDAQ: SBUX)	1992	$335,000
Sam Walton	Wal-Mart (NYSE: WMT)	1970	$60,000,000
Meg Whitman	eBay (NASDAQ: EBAY)	1998	$427,000

* Based on prices as of January 4, 2007

Finding Midas will teach you the following:

- How the Entrepreneurial CEO Investing approach works, and why

- Why most traditional investors fail over the long term
- Why the entrepreneurial CEO's significant ownership is so critical
- What to look for when researching the entrepreneurial CEO
- What to pay as a reasonable stock price
- How to determine when to stay with winners and when to dump the losers
- Why investors lost money during the recent corporate scandals
- How to avoid investing in the wrong entrepreneurial CEOs
- How to spot the best entrepreneurial CEOs
- How to apply the Entrepreneurial CEO Investing principles
- Why you must build a portfolio rather than invest in just one or two stocks

You will not want to wait to start applying this system to your own investment strategy because you will clearly see that the returns are incredible. To take a new twist on an old, yet appropriate slogan, the famous Fidelity fund portfolio manager and author, Peter Lynch, had a good quote, "It's not the stock market, stupid, it's the company," in explaining results. I believe another appropriate slogan is "It's not the stock market, stupid, it's the CEO."

As you read through the case studies in particular, you will see that incredible financial success came to the investors of these companies not because of the industry itself, but because of each company's CEO.

> *Entrepreneurial rich or poor determines*
> *whether a country is prosperous or not.*

About Entrepreneurship

Because this book concentrates on investing with Entrepreneurial CEOs, it would be good to define exactly what we mean when we use the term *entrepreneurial*. First, what is the difference between entrepreneurial management and professional management?

We believe entrepreneurial management concentrates on seeking new opportunities and trying to fulfill the needs of others. Entrepreneurialism is moving ahead with a clear vision, often with limited assets. An entrepreneur is an owner. Professional management is mostly about making assets more effective and efficient. Both types of management are important, but in our economy and the world economy, it is the entrepreneurs who create most of the economic growth and the wealth for everyone else.

This has been true over the past two hundred years. A small group of entrepreneurs in England began the industrial revolution by automating and mass-producing textiles. This continued in the United States through the efforts of such familiar names as Carnegie, Rockefeller, Edison, Ford, and Watson, to name a few. Entrepreneurs continue to drive the economic success of the United States today.

The new economic miracle of China is not the result of the government but the rising up of individual Chinese entrepreneurs. These people are creating great wealth for themselves, but they are also lifting up the entire Chinese economy. One of the best stories about this era is Dong Ying Hong, a poor teacher who was living in Datong, in northeast China, and making just $9 per month. She owned a sewing machine and began making socks—mainly because they wear out so fast. This turned out to be a good business to be in. Without any government help or direction, this provincial woman and her company now produce nearly 10 billion socks a year, about one-third of the world production. Her enterprise employs thousands of people and has made Dong Ying Hong a very wealthy woman.

Johan Norberg, author of *In Defense of Global Capitalism*, wrote an article in the October 2, 2006, edition of the *Wall Street Journal* in which he stated that entrepreneurs are "humanity's greatest achievement." He went on to speak about how little credit is given to the few who do so much for the many. In the United States, for example, 5 percent of the population pays 55 percent of the taxes! Almost all the new jobs in America are created by smaller, growing companies headed by entrepreneurs. As Norberg advised, "Thank entrepreneurs, not government, for prosperity."

Worldwide you can easily see those countries where entrepreneurs are succeeding and creating the highest growth rates.

China is in the lead, with India and certain Asian countries like Korea, Malaysia, Taiwan, and Japan also participating. Russia, Africa, Latin America, and even Europe are not experiencing rapid economic growth, due to a lack of entrepreneurs. For investors, the entrepreneurial economic climate in a country is the most important factor to consider. Entrepreneurial rich or poor determines whether a country is prosperous or not.

PART I:

THE PRINCIPLES OF ENTREPRENEURIAL CEO INVESTING

WAKE UP AND
BE RICH—FINDING
THE MEGA-STOCKS

Imagine investing a few thousand dollars and waking up several years later to find that your investments have generated a mega-fortune. This doesn't have to be wishful thinking.

It is incumbent upon the investor to do research beyond a stock's history and their broker's highly touted recommendations for its future. This is exactly what I've done for several years, and my own success has proven this to be the one critical factor that separates the winners from the losers.

WOULDN'T IT BE FUN to be like Rip van Winkle? Imagine investing a few thousand dollars and waking up twenty years later to find that your investments have generated a fortune. Further, imagine following a simple investment system that, once you've learned it and followed its basic principles, would enable you to no longer have to worry about the economy, the stock market, or any of the complex variables that so often preoccupy most investors.

Imagine, for example, that you had invested $100,000 and within twenty-five years it yielded you $10 million. Would that make you happy?

This doesn't have to be wishful thinking. You can actually do this. When company executives come in to talk to us, we look at a very specific checklist. Knowing that it's impossible to have everything on the list, we likewise know that the company doesn't have to meet all of the checklist criteria. It must have a high percentage of these characteristics, however, and when it does, it pays big dividends for us and our investors.

Now, in the pages of this book, we will share with you the same checklist that we use, as well as the principles and system by which you too can become a safe, profitable, and successful investor. We want to help make your long-term financial dreams come true.

Taking Responsibility

Investigation is an investor's responsibility: not just the professional investor, any investor. In saying this, we were not so naive as to think that average investors make their decisions after thorough investigation. Unfortunately, the reality is that some investors, even if they had investigated the character of a company's CEO, would have looked the other way as long as their investments were flourishing. Unrealistic returns had become what was expected. It's clear to us that few investors have the slightest idea that they, in part, are responsible for their own losses by failing to do the right kind of research. That means research into the people leading critical decisions—the CEOs.

Each investor must look beyond a stock's history and their broker's highly touted recommendations for its future. Instead, it is far more important to do some in-depth research to ensure that the company has the right CEO. This is exactly what we have done for several years, and our own success has proven this to be the one critical factor that separates the winners from the losers. Your trust in the market will be restored if you can learn what to look for in order to invest in the right CEO.

Why are we compelled to share this information with you? Because we want you to wake up and be rich and have the same opportunities to achieve wealth that we have had. The reality is that you can, if you can adjust your thinking to follow our lead and don't fall prey to the two traditional traps we elaborate on in the next chapter.

Your investigation should include looking for some very specific criteria. If a management company comes to RENN Capital Group to seek financing for its company, it receives the following summary of what we're looking for:

- CEO and management must have a major stake in the business

- A clear vision with above-average
  growth prospects
- Operations must be profitable
- Valuation must be reasonable

As you continue, you'll read our elaboration on each of these important criteria.

WAYS OF INVESTING

There is a better way!

IN INVESTING, you can follow many different investment strategies. We begin with short-term trading, a method through which you trade in and out every day or every week. There are many courses on this method; some are sold in infomercials on TV. While it is an intriguing idea, this daily or weekly trading in and out has not proven successful for most people. The brokers love it, but we always ask, How many traders are included on the Forbes 400 list of "The Wealthiest People in America"? To our knowledge, none.

In long-term investing there are a number of different strategies, most of which can produce results if followed correctly. The
first is called value investing. This strategy is to purchase only
those stocks that are selling near book value or at low price earnings ratios and to stay with them for a long period.

Another long-term strategy is called growth stock investing. Using this method you would buy shares only in companies
that are reporting high rates of growth in sales and earnings.
Usually, many of these stocks are selling at high prices in rela-
tion to earnings. There is a lot of risk here if you are wrong.
However, if a company continues to grow, significant gains can
be achieved.

An additional long-term trading strategy is called momentum growth. The idea here is to buy stocks that are making new
highs and stay with them until they begin to drop. Momentum
players seldom look at fundamentals; they mainly look at trading prices.

In recent years a strategy called hedging has become popular.
In this method you buy long certain stocks and sell short others
to hedge your bet. This method takes real skill, and we are not
sure of the long-term results.

There are other strategies, but these are the main ones.
You can be successful in any strategy if you know what you
are doing. Almost all successful strategies concern long-term
investing, so forget trying to get rich quick. In Entrepreneurial
CEO Investing, we are seeking long-term mega-gains using a
simple proven method.

Traditional Traps

Two major traps keep most investors from achieving results: (1) buying overvalued stocks, and (2) having a short-term mentality.

Overvalued Stocks

The single greatest loss for any investors, whether individual or professional, is when they buy into an industry fad near the top. A classic example of this was the Internet craze of the late 1990s into the year 2000. This craze was undoubtedly the single greatest loss to investors in history. The NASDAQ Stock Market, the Exchange in which most of these companies traded, dropped from a high of 5048 in March 2000 to 1114 in October 2002. This is a decline of nearly 80 percent. For a while the Internet industry appeared to be fast flying, and the reality is that fast birds don't fly far. Day-trading became as common then as instant messaging is now. But, when the Internet industry came crashing down, unrealistic expectations and lack of proper investigation proved fatal for many investor bank accounts.

The key to mega-stock investing is focusing not on the industry but rather on the entrepreneurial leadership characteristics of the CEO. That's why mega-stock results can come from such diverse industries as airlines (a disaster for most investors), mortgage credit, discount stores, auto parts, and conglomerates with concentrations in insurance, as well as such growth industries as computers and software.

Short-term Mentality

In a quest to make big gains, too many investors have a short-term mentality. They focus on what gains they can make as quickly as possible, as opposed to thinking about the really big, longer-term gains that could be happening behind the scenes. By making a quick small profit, investors with a short-term mentality forsake the mega-profits; they think, unrealistically, that what worked on a few quick trades can be duplicated again and again. These kinds of investors might just as well shoot craps in Las Vegas, where the odds of coming out ahead of the house are just about the same.

THERE IS A BETTER WAY

To help you avoid falling prey to these fatal investment flaws, it is important for you to begin to view your investing through a new set of eyes.

We don't have much opportunity to spend time with these CEOs, but we can make judgments about people by observing them under controlled conditions, looking for telling responses, and developing decision rules based on past experiences. The best place to begin is to look at their percentage of ownership. Ownership trumps all else.

SIGNIFICANT OWNERSHIP

Many years ago the British and the Dutch owned a number of sugar plantations in the Caribbean. The plantations seemed to be very successful while the owners were around, but when it got too hot and the owners decided to go back to England or Europe for a year or two, lo and behold, the natives took over the plantations. You see, the hired hands decided that since there was no one around to supervise them, they would just take the wealth into their own hands.

In a similar vein, this scenario reminds me of what happens when you go into a restaurant whose owner is there to greet you and to supervise the operations. There is a great difference between the quality of service at the time the owner is there and when the owner is gone. It makes sense that ownership makes a difference—a huge difference. So, the first criterion for selecting stocks is to invest only in companies where the chief executive officer—and possibly even his management team—has significant stock ownership of the company.

When you are looking at small companies, the CEO should have enough stock ownership to realize a significant fortune if the company is successful. On the other hand, his investment should be significant enough that if he fails at managing the company, it will hurt him as much or more than any shareholder in the company. It should come as no surprise that history shows that where CEOs are major shareholders, companies do considerably better than others where CEOs have little personal financial commitment. Thus, the premise of our book—and it's not just we who have come to this conclusion.

Boston management consultant Jack Dolmat-Connell has conducted a number of surveys in which he looked at stock ownership versus option granting. In one such survey he looked at

144 companies in ten different industries. What he found came as no surprise to us. The top-performing companies tend to have executives with high ratios of real stock ownership as opposed to stock options.

An interesting ratio results from dividing the value of the stock owned by the salary of the executive. When the stock is worth considerably more than their salaries, the executives tend to do very well. Among those Dolmat-Connell pointed to as examples were Southwest Airlines, where there was a significant ownership, versus Delta Airlines, where there were executives who had mainly been given stock options. He also found this factor to run across almost every industry group, from pharmaceuticals and banking to computers and beverage makers, etc.

In his practice Dolmat-Connell has been advocating that companies stop using stock options as a method of reward. Instead, he recommends they switch to restricted stock grants or create programs in which executives actually become real owners of the company, not simply spectators sitting on the sidelines.

Looking back you will see that the dot.com bubble burst was driven in part by the short-term lure of options. Later in this book we will discuss some of the false prophet CEOs at such seemingly good firms to invest in as Enron, WorldCom, and others, and how the fact that they had too many options and too little ownership contributed to the debacles that eventually took place.

How Much Ownership?

The next question becomes, How much ownership should a CEO have? I believe that the CEO's absolute minimum ownership should be in the 5 to 10 percent range. The specific amount will depend greatly on the growth cycle of the company and whether the company has matured. As a company grows and raises more capital in the equity markets, it is natural for the original investment of the CEO to become diluted and for his interest to go down even though, if the company is financially successful, his total net worth is going up.

The CEO's personal equity investment in the company becomes a measure of the nature and extent of his commitment to the company. Unlike a mere stock option, a significant personal equity investment provides the CEO with a significant financial responsibility and reward for generating positive results for the shareholders. At the same time, it imposes a significant penalty for negative results. The personal investment demonstrates an intensity of belief that is instantly communicated to every individual in the organization. It should send an equally strong message to potential investors.

The whole concept of owning equity in the company is not much different from owning equity in your home. If the value of your house goes up, you make a profit. If the value goes down, you lose. Likewise, if the stock price goes up, the owners (the CEO and the other shareholders) make a profit. Or, if the stock price goes down, the owners lose money. Thus, when the CEO has his own money heavily invested in the company, it makes sense that as a primary owner he is motivated to keep the value of the company up and he is willing to work hard to do so. Ownership simply motivates the vested manager to invest and manage wisely.

Here's a scary thought. When you think about how much a CEO may have invested in the company that he leads, think about this: many corporate CEOs have more money at risk in their own homes than they do in the companies they lead.

Ownership Versus Stock Options

From an ownership standpoint, there is a very, very important distinction between a CEO investing his own money and a CEO being given stock options. When you look at the proxy of any given company, it will show how much stock the CEO and other key executives own. But if you look carefully at the fine print, you will find out that most of the stock is actually owned through stock options that have been granted to these individuals. Often, these individuals don't exercise their options, but they do nevertheless have the option. A common example would be the option to buy 500,000 shares at a stipulated price.

In theory, the philosophy is that if you give the CEO and the rest of the executive team a certain amount of shares and they work to increase the stock price, then they can make their options worth more money and in that way provide benefit to the shareholders. Now, contrast that with someone who has actually used his own money to buy shares and actually has put "skin in the game." Therein lies the difference. When the CEO invests his own money and actually buys shares, it is hugely different from when it appears he has 500,000 shares that are, in reality, only optioned to him but never actually paid for. Those shares are like a gift from the shareholders and not at all like shares that individuals have actually invested in with their own money. Therefore, it is critical that you look at shares bought with the CEO's own money, versus options that have been granted to him, when you're trying to determine the CEO's real commitment to his company.

Control Determines Leadership

The reason this distinction is so important is that the quality and direction of leadership that emerge in a small public corporation are a perfect reflection of the attitudes, desires, and motivations of the stockholders who elect its directors and of the directors who appoint its officers. This electoral process is almost always dominated by a very small number of individuals—typically by one person who may or may not have the title of CEO.

In the classic situation, the controlling person is an individual who founded the company, built it up, and sold stock to others—private investors first, then the public—but retained enough to control the direction of the company. The founder typically remains active in management for many years but may gradually withdraw, choosing to exercise control from behind the scenes. In other cases, the controlling person may be an investor who has bought a significant interest in the company, or he could be an individual with little or no stock who by reputation and political skill commands a majority vote of the directors and shareholders.

Caution is needed when a company divides control or there is no apparent controlling person at all. Companies with no apparent controlling person tend to drift from strategy to strategy as control passes from one clique of shareholders to another. Companies with divided control get bogged down in internal conflict, and in such situations decisive response to significant challenges or opportunities is unlikely. This has happened to many U.S. companies.

From an internal perspective, small emerging public companies are miniature autocracies. The controlling person has the votes, and the votes bring absolute authority over all internal affairs. Legitimate authority generates respect, and business success brings loyalty.

I think of such companies as airplanes. The fuselage and wings are the organizational structure, and the engines are the sales. The passengers are the investors. Employees, customers, and suppliers are along for the ride. The controlling person—the individual with the votes—is the pilot. The weather forecast calls for rough weather, wind, and rain. Some planes will reach their destinations safely; some will not. Selection of the right pilot is the most important factor to guarantee the success of the flight.

Using this airplane metaphor we realize that no sane person would board an airplane that didn't have a competent pilot, but relied on a committee of pilots, or had a student pilot flying alone. In the air we all recognize that it is imperative for someone to be responsible; someone must be available to resolve problems or conflict quickly. We want that person to be as well trained, experienced, and committed as possible. No sane person would board an airplane with the intention of hiring a new pilot from the outside once the plane is in the air, and no sane person would board an airplane planning to bail out if he didn't like the way the pilot flew the plane. We would check out the pilot before taking off. Likewise, we should check out the CEO before we invest.

In the world of aviation we are able to rely on a vast training industry, government agencies, and the airlines themselves to ensure that only qualified pilots fly the planes we board. But in the investment world, we are on our own. No standardized tests or guidelines are available by which to judge a CEO's competency. Therefore we must improvise and create standards on our own. Just what should we look for?

Unfortunately, no one publishes the results of "flight checks" of small company CEOs. From a distance they all look similar. So, can an ordinary investor investigate these issues and make rational investment decisions? The work of a World War II psychiatrist named Eric Berne gives us a framework to consider. During the later days of the war Berne was inducted into the U.S. Army fresh from his residency. He was given the rank of major and told to devise a system to evaluate the mental health of every individual to be discharged from the U.S. military in the city of Chicago. He thought he'd been assigned a dream job until he realized he would have merely one and a half minutes to spend with each person to make his determination. If he made a mistake he might release a homicidal sociopath or, conversely, keep a healthy person unfairly trapped in military service. There were no existing guidelines. He was on his own.

With considerable thought Berne successfully developed a process by which he could accurately evaluate the mental health of an individual in ninety seconds: he simply carefully observed each person's response to a controlled environment and asked two or three questions. He applied his process to hundreds of thousands of people, with few mistakes, and went on to found the important discipline called Transactional Analysis. He then wrote a book, based on his process, titled *Games People Play*, which became a best seller in the 1970s. At the end of his long professional life Berne wrote that the most important tool you can have in evaluating people is your own intuition.

The problem we, as investors, have—and our solution—is conceptually similar to that of Eric Berne. We don't have the ability to gather all the information we would like to have, and there are no tried-and-true measurements to follow. We don't have much opportunity to spend time with these CEOs, but we can make judgments about people by observing them under controlled conditions, looking for telling responses, and developing decision rules based on past experiences. The best place to begin is to look at their percentage of ownership. The next qualifier we will want to look at is leadership strategy and vision—the topic of our next chapter. But even before leadership, never forget that the CEO's personal equity investment in the company will be the greatest measure of the nature and extent to which he is committed to the company. Ownership trumps all else.

LEADING WITH CLEAR STRATEGY AND VISION

"If your actions inspire others to dream more, learn more, do more, and become more, you are a leader."

—John Quincy Adams

IF THERE'S ONE THING successful CEOs have done that can be looked to from a prospective investment standpoint, it's that they have a clear strategy. Equally important, they are able to spread that strategy throughout the organization to the point where the employees, the board of directors, and everyone associated with the company all clearly know how they fit into the organization and understand the purpose and intentions to perform. When this clarity is firm, great things can happen. When it's not, the company's mission can become blurred and its employees unfocused.

A recent example of this lack of clarity and its results is K-Mart. Just walking into a K-Mart you can sense what we would call a "whipped dog" attitude among employees, as compared to the positive attitude among the friendly, helpful, and focused people working at a Wal-Mart. Much of this can be attributed to a management that failed to clearly articulate a strategy everyone could grasp and believe in. By contrast, Sam Walton was a very strong leader whose Wal-Mart employees knew exactly what his intentions were.

Southwest Airlines is another great example of the success that comes from having and communicating a clear strategy. Herb Kelleher set out his precise strategy from the beginning: Southwest would not be an airline that would fly 747s overseas or would serve areas requiring direct long-haul flights. Instead, it was clearly communicated that Southwest would be an airline that would focus on commuter-oriented flights, with an emphasis on quality service, quick turnaround, and low fares. This clear strategy stands in sharp contrast to the confusion and lack of harmony created by a number of the major airlines, particularly those that failed to survive, such as Trans World Airlines, Pan American, and Eastern.

The big question, of course, is, How do we determine whether the CEO has a clear and focused strategy that has been sufficiently communicated to the rest of the organization? In most cases you can find the answer easily by reading the company's annual report; it will become quite clear whether the company has deviated or is deviating from its original core strategy.

When we talk about Entrepreneurial CEO Investing, we are focusing on the major lightning rod—the CEO. We must also keep in mind, however, that it is a team of people who will take the actions necessary to achieve ultimate success. In that regard, *the successful CEO will have the capability of building a team of people who will follow his leadership by flawlessly executing the strategy that he has developed. The CEO will build a culture of focus and performance.*

THE LEADERSHIP ROLE

The principles of leadership are timeless. They can be found at the core of virtually every successful enterprise, yet they are virtually ignored by every security analyst and stock market professional. Conventional wisdom may say that, in retrospect, effective leadership is obvious. But is it? In retrospect it always looks like it was easy. It's easy to hypothesize that all successful growth companies just happened to have a great idea at the right time, and when the world recognized it, that was it. Wrong. In reality great ideas seldom arise suddenly, in a vacuum, all by themselves. Great ideas come from multiple people, often at the same time. Virtually every successful growth company in history has emerged from a crowd of competitors, many with like ideas.

Berkshire Hathaway was hardly alone in its business in 1965. Warren Buffett competed with a host of colorful characters, all of whom received more coverage in the investment press at the time, but most of whom have now been forgotten.

At lease four retail discount store chains were organized in 1962: Woolco, K-Mart, Target, and Wal-Mart. Wal-Mart was founded by a small operator in a small town in northwestern Arkansas; the other three were sponsored by large, experienced retailers. Yet by 1999, Wal-Mart's sales were more than $127 billion, compared to K-Mart's $37 billion. No element recognized by traditional security analysts explains why Wal-Mart emerged strongly from the pack. Could it have been leadership and the leadership's strategy and vision? You bet.

LEADERSHIP MAKES THE DIFFERENCE

As in any system or method of investing, the closer you can come to defining and quantifying leadership characteristics, the better your decision making will be. Our checklist to use when looking at companies in which to invest is not totally engraved in stone, but it is a way of coming up with a score to evaluate any given company by and to determine the viability of an investment. This checklist provides a basis for taking an objective view of a portfolio company, and it begins with the CEO.

Invest only in companies in which you can clearly understand the strategy of the CEO and can see that this strategy has been communicated sufficiently to have permeated the entire organization. Is the company profitable and does it have a growing business process?

By a successful business process we mean creating sales, controlling costs, and generating profits.

MORE THAN AN EDUCATION

Don't focus too much on how highly educated the CEO is. Often, the most successful entrepreneurs are self-educated rather than college educated, and they do not rely on advice from Ph.D.s in any one specific area. For example, although Bill Gates, the greatest technological CEO of the twentieth century, was admitted to Harvard, he never finished. You can go down the list of CEOs and find that occasionally one or two of them may have graduated from Harvard Business School or the Wharton School, but by and large, there is no correlation between an Ivy League education and success in business. In fact, many of the most successful CEOs, while they may have college degrees, actually derive their applicable knowledge from the fact that they are lifetime students. They have great curiosity and they apply the practical insights they learn through experience and life to achieve their company's greatest growth and success.

INHERITED POWER

Another factor that is often considered integral to success is inheritance. Some think that people who inherit a lot of money are more destined for success. In reality, most of the truly successful CEOs did not come from wealthy families. On the contrary, the most successful entrepreneurs often worked their way through college. Frequently the fact that they did not come from a wealthy base actually motivated them to work hard to achieve their goals.

INDUSTRY SYNDROME

I call this "the jockey or the horse philosophy." One of the most interesting things about CEO investing I have found to be absolute truth is that it is the jockey who seems to find the right horse to ride rather than the industry that finds the right jockey. If the jockey has a horse that's not working, he recognizes the situation and gets another horse. It is for this very reason that we find great successes in industries where nearly every one else has failed. These are the instances where it is the superb strategy and insight of the jockey that take the horse across the winning finish line. Where there is no vision there is no progress.

THERE ARE ONLY
TWO TYPES OF CEOs
IN WHOM TO INVEST

"There are only two types of CEOs in whom to invest: those who make money, and those who do not. Pick those who do."

—Bill Bowen

SOME YEARS AGO Bill Bowen, a very successful investor, was involved in a partnership with Russell Cleveland. When Bowen died several years ago he had amassed a considerable fortune, starting with only a modest investment. One of Bowen's favorite expressions was "There are only two types of managers in this world: those who make money, and those who do not." I have added the following to this slogan: "In the investment business it is better to associate with those who make money."

One of the most interesting things you will find as you study Entrepreneurial CEO Investing is that the really successful CEOs did not start companies that had financial losses for years before they became profitable. One of the big fallacies of the last twenty to twenty-five years is that a company must lose a lot of money as it develops its markets and then, all of a sudden, it will become profitable when it obtains a certain level of sales. We believe that part of this myth has been perpetuated by the Japanese and is a philosophy that became somewhat the darling of many business schools—the market share concept. The premise is, you lose a lot of money and develop a market share that's better than anyone else's, then, using this dominant position, you can control prices and thus make a profit.

Personally, we believe this is one of the most unsuccessful strategies we have ever heard of. Consider this. If you look at a market growth graph you will find that the Japanese stock market is down about 80 percent from where it was fourteen years ago. And the Japanese, of course, were the leading proponents of this type of approach.

Every time a CEO starts talking to us about having to reach a certain sales level to become profitable, we know not to invest. Just ask yourself this simple question: Do you think Bill Gates and Sam Walton ever lost millions of dollars getting their businesses under way?

The primary reason why most investors lost a great deal of money during the speculative boom of the late '90s into 2000 was that these companies were not profitable. In fact, many were not even growing. They were simply promotions based on this idiotic "market share" or "space" concept, and many gullible investors fell into the trap and huge losses resulted.

One statement floating around Wall Street among value investors advises to "buy only what *is* rather than what *if*." So, let's make this very clear. You would invest only in a CEO who already has a growing profitable business process in place. You're not going to guess that this company is going to become profitable. You're not going to believe the Wall Street stories. But you're going to have to be disciplined and view the investment criteria very, very carefully. This means you would simply not invest in a company that is not profitable.

You may say, "Well, this is going to come." But again, your chance of winning here is extremely low, as compared to a company having a clear investment strategy based on all the elements of the Entrepreneurial CEO Investing concept. Remember, there are only two types of CEOs in whom to invest: those who make money, and those who do not. Pick those who do.

A REASONABLE PRICE

> You don't have to have a tremendous education in valuations or be a Chartered Financial Analyst. You do have to understand that most great winners occur from two standpoints: Earnings are going up and sales are going up. But . . . what is the price earnings ratio?

WHAT IS A REASONABLE PRICE to pay for a company's stock? This is an area that always seems to be difficult for many investors, and it's one that often separates the men from the boys. You can have satisfied all the criteria we've talked about for a successful CEO—significant ownership in the company, a clear strategy, and a profitable process—and still, if you are going to overpay for the stock, your chance for an above-average gain goes down considerably.

Ironically, the investing public has usually been right about the long-term directions of industries in the past 150 years. The recent overvaluation in the Internet and technology arena was no exception. We have little doubt that the Internet will be a hugely successful area overall, and that vast fortunes will be made relating to it. But it's important to realize that within this industry the public was buying companies that were *losing* $50 million a year, yet they had $5 to $10 billion market valuations (market capitalizations). Even with a really successful venture like John Chambers and Cisco, the problem was that the valuation got so inflated there was only one way for the stock to go—down. At one point Cisco had the highest valuation of any company in the world: more than General Electric, IBM, and AT&T. So, to be successful in using the Entrepreneurial CEO Investing criteria, you must also be sure to buy the company's stock at a reasonable price.

And just how does someone determine whether a stock's price is reasonable or not?

Take the sales revenues of the company and compare that figure to the market capitalization of the company. This is fairly easy to do. These valuations can be found in most stock research services. All you need to know are the number of shares that are outstanding and the stock's current price. Multiply these two figures. For example, if the company's stock is trading at $10 per share and there are 10 million shares outstanding (owned), the market capitalization (market value) is $100 million.

Market capitalization, which is often abbreviated to "market cap," is the term used to refer to the overall value of a company's stock—the price one must pay to buy an entire company. The size and growth of a company's market cap is often one of the most critical measurements of a public company's success or failure. As we've just demonstrated, market capitalization is calculated by multiplying the number of shares of the company that are outstanding by the current price of those shares.

Another aspect you must examine is the debt of the company. Using our example above, if the company has $100 million of debt, that figure must be added to the $100 million market cap to give you a total value, which in this case is $200 million.

The way we use these values is to ask ourselves as business professionals, If a company has a value of $200 million, what would be a reasonable price for shares in this business? We would look at the sales revenues of the company and if, for example, the sales are $100 million, then we would say the example price of $10 per share is reasonable. If, on the other hand, the company's market cap is $100 million and it has only $10 million in revenues, we would seriously question $10 per share being a reasonable price.

Reasonable doesn't necessarily mean cheap. Many of the really successful companies never sold at an extremely low valuation in relationship to earnings, book value, etc. You don't have to have a tremendous education in valuations or be a Chartered Financial Analyst to be knowledgeable. What is important to understand is that most great winners arrive at success from two standpoints: earnings are going up, and sales are going up.

It is also important to realize, however, that what people are willing to pay for a company's stock is growing at a much higher rate of sales and earnings. For example, one of the terms we use in analysis is *price earnings ratio*. To determine price earnings ratio, simply take the price of the stock and divide it by the earnings. For example, if a stock is $10 per share and the earnings per share are $1, this stock's price to earnings ratio would be ten, or ten times its earnings.

Price earnings ratios for both the market and individual companies will vary greatly over time. But obviously, if you can buy stock in a company that is growing rapidly—but is only selling at ten times its earnings—and the price earnings ratios continue to go up, then your chance of realizing superior gains becomes much better.

Take our illustration of the $10 stock. If the price earnings ratio went to twenty, you would have a $20 stock. If it went to thirty, forty, fifty, you would have the same company but at thirty, forty, or fifty times its earnings. At the fifty point, your stock would be $50 rather than $10, or five times higher.

You can clearly see how this works and that this is where a lot of appreciation occurs. So, as an investor, you want to be on the more reasonable side of these valuations in order to benefit when the market begins to identify the CEO and the company as showing great potential for growth.

Among the greatest proponents of value investing, along with a number of other techniques, is Warren Buffett, who by following simple valuation principles with discipline became the wealthiest man in America.

Finally, understand that successful CEOs and their growing companies will probably not be selling at bargain basement prices, so this valuation is a relative term. Nevertheless, it is an important one, and for you to be totally successful in using the Entrepreneurial CEO Investment strategy, you must think about a reasonable price in relationship to the other criteria that we've outlined.

The main principle to keep in mind: invest in companies that are reasonably priced at the time you buy into them.

APPLYING
THE PRINCIPLES:
A SYSTEM FOR FINDING
THE MEGA-STOCKS

> All the knowledge in the world will do little if you do not use it.

IN JUNE 2001 principals from Select Comfort came by to see us. The company produces a revolutionary air mattress and has been in business for a number of years. Select Comfort had over-expanded and lost its way by 2001. The stock, which had once seen a high of $30 a share, had plummeted to as low as 80 cents a share. In an attempt to turn the company around, its board of directors hired a new CEO—William McLaughlin. McLaughlin, whose background offered nothing related to selling mattresses, had been running the overseas sales operations of a national soft drink company. He did bring fresh thinking to Select Comfort, however, and immediately began to look for a new way of marketing.

With input from advertising specialists, McLaughlin came up with a new idea that would use a "sleep number" as the basis for the marketing campaign instead of the orthopedic-oriented "get a good night's rest and alleviate back and neck problems" strategy that had been stressed previously. The new sleep number campaign called for using a handheld monitor that would change the amount of air pressure from, say, 10 to 20 pounds of air to as much as 100 pounds. The individual could then select whatever sleep number felt best. Furthermore, if the individual had a king-size bed, his/her partner could select his/her own number, which could be completely different, guaranteeing a personalized comfort level for them both.

As part of the marketing concept McLaughlin began using known personalities, including popular news commentator Paul Harvey and conservative talk show host Rush Limbaugh, as Select Comfort's main spokespeople in radio commercials. Once the radio commercials began to produce results, McLaughlin expanded the campaign by adding a whole series of television ads, all focused around the sleep number concept. The turnaround success was very impressive, but that was not the main reason that convinced us to invest in the company.

What did? It was when we asked McLaughlin whether he was personally willing to invest if we put a million dollars into Select Comfort. His response was matter of fact. Without hesitation McLaughlin said he would match us with a personal million-dollar investment. At that moment, Select Comfort moved to the top of our investment list. Not only did the company have a proven product and a successful new marketing campaign, more importantly we had a CEO who was totally committed to the company with both his talents and his own money.

In two years' time Select Comfort's stock advanced to twenty-eight times our investment. Had you joined us, investing just $10,000 in the summer of 2001, two years later that small investment would have turned into $280,000. Or, if you had invested $100,000, you would have become a millionaire, because that investment would have turned into $2.8 million.

Think about it. We're not talking about some new high-tech product making us millions. We're talking about a somewhat ordinary, everyday product that has all kinds of competitors in the marketplace, but its company is led by a CEO with innovative, visionary thinking and a willingness to invest in his own thinking. The key consideration here was McLaughlin's joining the company with a commitment to become a significant investor, then being innovative in leading the company to outstanding results. This is a clear example of the incredible power of Entrepreneurial CEO Investing.

In each and every one of the cases you've read about thus far (and will further see in the case studies in part II), it was the CEO and his investment, vision, and decision making that had a dramatic impact on the growth of the company and, thus, its stock. These are the companies in which mega-returns were possible. Never was the financial growth about the industry itself.

Collectively, the authors of this book and their business partners have invested in literally hundreds of publicly owned companies. They have also operated all types of funds. Yet, about 90 percent of the investments have been in small companies whose indicators signaled they would grow rapidly. That philosophy has given us a very successful track record over a very long period of time. In recent years, we've solely focused on applying the many principles of Entrepreneurial CEO Investing to our portfolios.

To demonstrate the power of Entrepreneurial CEO Investing, we thought it would be good to move beyond the discussion of successful CEOs and fast-forward to an example of our own recent successes with this concept. You will clearly see it was the impact of the CEO, not the industry itself, which provided these mega-growth opportunities.

TAKING ACTION ON MEDICAL ACTION

From time to time we encounter CEO investment opportunities by attending a variety of investment conferences. Such was the case several years ago when we attended a conference in New York City and heard a presentation by Paul Meringolo, of Medical Action.

Meringolo cofounded the company with a brother who has since left the business. Their goal was to specialize in disposable products to be used in hospital operating rooms (ORs). Medical

Action began as a small provider of sponges and allied equipment for ORs and gradually expanded into a number of other disposable medical products. The key issue was that Meringolo was a significant shareholder, owning approximately 25 percent of the company. Even after the company went public, he was not tempted to sell his shares in the open market and pull his profits; instead, he held on to his stock.

At the time we became acquainted with Medical Action, its stock was selling for approximately $3 per share, with revenues of about $30 million. As of January 2007, the company is generating revenues in excess of $100 million, with an excellent profit margin. After languishing for years with little interest except among a few visionaries who saw its potential, the stock has gone as high as $33 a share.

This company met all the criteria for Entrepreneurial CEO Investing. The CEO owned a significant stake in the business, and he was a visionary who had the talent to enter a relatively large industry and succeed at gaining a share of the market. All the while shares were selling at very reasonable prices. So, for us, this was a classic CEO play. Along the line we have taken some profits and have added to our positions. We believe this company warrants our being long-time investors.

Our point is this: the information we are sharing with you is truly an investment system that we not only believe in but also put to work in our own everyday decisions. If you were to research the winning companies we've chosen, you would see that most of the ideas for starting the companies originated with the current CEO, and that that same CEO is a significant shareholder.

Laserscope is a good example from our own successful portfolio of a key individual within a company advancing into the CEO position. Eric Reuter was the chief technology officer of this company, bringing a strong technical background in lasers to the forefront. When the company lost its way, Reuter took over the CEO role and began to move the company forward. Through his vision and innovative ideas, Reuter added a new revolutionary technique in which green lasers are used for the treatment of enlarged prostates. This innovation addresses a very important area of medicine, particularly because of an aging population in which millions of men are faced with prostate issues. This new procedure won widespread acceptance because it overtakes other, less effective or painful treatments.

Reuter's vision and leadership put the company into position for major growth. In July 2006 American Medical purchased Laserscope for $31 per share. A $3.9 million investment by Renaissance Funds resulted in gains of $79 million over a four-year period.

Sometimes a Turnaround

Most of the major winning companies related to Entrepreneurial CEO Investing were built from ideas that originated with the CEO of the company and that, of course, is why he is a significant shareholder.

Occasionally, however, you will find that you will begin with a turnaround in which the new man, somewhat like the CEO of Select Comfort, will be either advanced or brought in. He may not have a significant amount of shares at the start, but he is given options, and earns shares, and over a period of time becomes a very substantial shareholder.

We realize that like most of the examples we've provided, you can only know the report card by looking back and seeing in hindsight whether the CEO was the kind of person you thought he was. It is often difficult to see CEOs as they are right at the moment of investigation; it's very hard to be sure you will pick out the next Bill Gates of the world.

The following checklist is a way of coming up with a total number so that you can have a more objective view of the portfolio company you're considering investing in.

All the knowledge in the world will do little if you do not use it. We suggest using this simple checklist to guide you in making your Entrepreneurial CEO Investing selections. A passing grade is a score of at least 75 points. Using this system, you would not select any company whose score was less than 75 points. Ideally you would invest only in companies with an Entrepreneurial CEO Investing score near 100.

ENTREPRENEURIAL CEO INVESTING CHECKLIST

	Total Possible Points	Your Score
1. CEO ownership		
a. Less than 5%	0	_____
b. 5–10%	25	_____
c. More than 10%	35	_____
2. A clear corporate strategy	0–15	_____
3. Profitable, growing business	0–25	_____
4. Reasonable price capitalization (*stock market price times shares outstanding, compared to revenues*)		
a. Less than one times revenues	25	_____
b. One to two times revenues	20	_____
c. Three times revenues	15	_____
d. Over three times revenues	5	_____
e. Over four times revenues	0	_____
Total Points		_____

DIVERSIFICATION

> "We see the past clearly but unfortunately we live in the future. The world is perfectly imperfect."
>
> —from *The Lazy Man's Guide to Enlightenment*
>
> ---
>
> How many different positions do you need to be successful? I like the rule of ten.

BY NOW, WE HOPE YOU CAN SEE that the Entrepreneurial CEO Investing system is by far the best way to accumulate a substantial portfolio. The system is no better than its practitioner, however, and like all systems, there is never 100 percent success. No matter how smart or good you are at picking just one company, certain forces will, for some reason, determine it is the one company that does not turn out to produce the way you would have liked. Consequently, the Entrepreneurial CEO Investing system—or any method of investing—requires diversification to make it work effectively.

The big question is, How many different positions do you need in order to be successful? We like the rule of ten. This rule says that you must have at least ten different positions to have adequate diversification. For example, if you start with a fund of $100,000, you would invest $10,000 in each of ten different companies. If you wanted to be even more conservative (because the gains in this system are so large, and you want to cover more potential companies), you could expand that diversification to fifteen or twenty companies. So, if you chose to invest in twenty companies, continuing with the example above, you would buy five thousand dollars' worth of stock in each company.

One of the laws that we've followed over the years is the Pareto principle, which was formulated in the early 1900s. The Pareto principle states that 80 percent of the results you see will come from 20 percent of your effort. Applying this to portfolio management, 80 percent of your gains will come from 20 percent of your portfolio. Let's use an illustration.

We have ten stocks in our portfolio in which we've invested $10,000 each. According to the Pareto principle, we are expecting 80 percent of our profit to come from $20,000 of this investment ($10,000 × 2). If we made $1 million on those two investments, it would mean that that $20,000 would yield a long-term portfolio of $2 million-plus. It could be that you do considerably better than this, but we're just pointing out the 80/20 rule because in any stage, one of the main objectives is to be realistic about what you have.

Human nature being what it is, people always want us to pick one or two stocks for them from our "favorites." Ironically, if we mention only one or two stocks, these will be the underperformers. So, to be successful in Entrepreneurial CEO Investing you must have a portfolio—not just one or two favorites. Yet never forget that most of your gains will most likely come from just two to three of those holdings. If you hit 50 percent you will be beating most of the professionals. The big thing here is staying with winners and selling losers. Consequently, the next chapter is as important as anything you will ever read.

STAYING WITH WINNERS

There will be enormous pressure for you to sell your winners. Don't you sell them!

REGARDLESS of what investment system you use, there's one principle that makes a lot of sense, yet for most people it seems to be very difficult to follow. That principle is simply to stay with the winners and sell the losers.

Most people who invest in the stock market take their small profits and keep stocks in which they've had losses such that, in the end, their total return over the years is very poor. What you will find out about investing, if you haven't already, is that there is a lot of pressure and there are a lot of myths that you will have to totally ignore if you are going to make the kind of huge gains possible from the Entrepreneurial CEO Investing system.

The first myth you will hear from brokers, and others, is: *You never go broke taking a profit.* The problem with this myth is that in order to do this you will actually be selling the winners. You will sell yourself out of the company with the super-CEO. And you will find this is extremely easy to do.

To be successful in the Entrepreneurial CEO Investing system you are going to have to tell everybody you are associated with that you are not a short-term trader. In fact, you are one of the longest-term investors they will probably ever know, and you're not interested in their advice on getting out of something when you know you have the right CEO.

One of the interesting things we've observed in the market is that, usually, 90 percent of the stock moves occur only 10 percent of the time. In other words, if you are invested in a company for twenty years, 90 percent of that time—or eighteen years—you will see little movement, and the days when the stock is actually running up will constitute just a couple of years. Now, those eighteen years when the stock has little movement can seem like a long period of time, but you can have periods when the stocks do nothing. Or, perhaps the market is a bear market. Amid such fluctuations the main criterion that remains consistent is the CEO and his management. When you have made the right selection based on the CEO, you don't have to worry about the quiet times or the panicky times.

Another investment system states: *If a stock doubles, take most of your money out and then play for free with the rest.* The problem is that when you are using the Entrepreneurial CEO Investing system, you *want* to stay with your big winners. If you are selling half of your position, or a third of your position, you are going to miss a lot of the great gains that are possible. Now, obviously, if you make a million dollars on a $10,000 investment, you may at some point want to sell your original $10,000 and do other things with that money. But if you get tempted by the world to sell your position—and there is incredible pressure to take your profits and run—you could be robbed of great potential profits.

If you decide to follow the Entrepreneurial CEO Investing system and begin to win big in single stocks, there will be enormous pressure for you to sell your winners. This pressure will come from stockbrokers, investment counselors, attorneys, family, friends—maybe even your dog barking—all of whom are well meaning, but way off the mark. Our advice—Don't You Sell It!

Advice to Avoid

1. "You never go broke taking a profit."
   Don't you sell it!
2. "Diversification is prudent, sell now."
   Don't you sell it!
3. "The economy is weak."
   Don't you sell it!

4. "The stock market is going to crash."
   Don't you sell it!
5. "You need a new car or home."
   Don't you sell it!

Stay with the winners! Remember, you are investing with and in winning entrepreneurial CEOs—stay with them.

The opposite side of this coin is getting out of losers. According to Entrepreneurial CEO Investing, when you sell losers you would replace them with new investments.

When looking to sell, keep in mind that the chief reason we invested in these companies was the CEO and his strategy and leadership. The key criteria we used were whether the CEO is a major owner of the business and whether the company is profitable and growing. Obviously, if you see that the CEO is selling most of his stock, for whatever reasons, then it's time for you to join him and sell most of your stock.

We're not talking about the CEO who takes a modest amount to set up a trust or something of this nature for charity or others. This is commonly done by a number of very successful CEOs. We're talking about when the CEO sells his core positions and bails out. This is a huge red flag. And, under a new Securities and Exchange Commission (SEC) ruling, the CEO must file within three days of either buying or selling. So, you need to be alert to when the CEO starts to sell.

WHEN TO SELL

> When you see a large percentage of the CEO's shares being sold—you had better join him.

THE MAIN THESIS of Entrepreneurial CEO Investing is to join as investor with the CEO and "ride the horse" a long way. This is where your best chance for mega-gains is to be found.

The question becomes, When do I sell and take profits?

Death or Retirement

The first rule is to sell when the entrepreneurial CEO dies or retires. Usually, the strong momentum of leadership can carry the stock higher for several years after the CEO leaves, but the mega-gains are generally over. While there is no rush to sell, when the main jockey is no longer riding the horse, it is time to let go. Take your profits, pay your taxes, and be happy!

If you examine the history of many of the great mega-growth stocks of the past fifty years, you will find that the golden era was when the entrepreneurial leadership was present. You will find this to be true of such well-known companies as Texas Instruments, Hewlett-Packard, Intel, McDonalds, and Xerox, to name a few. This would now apply to Wal-Mart as well.

CEO Sell Out

The next red flag to look for is when you find the CEO selling large blocks of his stock in the company. Under SEC law, senior-level management must file a Form 4 within three days of either buying or selling shares in their company. This information is readily available on Bloomberg or any other electronic service and from any stockbroker. A number of investment services, which you can purchase, also provide this information. Let us repeat that we are not speaking about the CEO selling a modest amount of his shares for personal reasons. When you see a CEO selling a large percentage of his shares, however, you had better join him and sell your shares too. People tend to act in their own personal best interest, so you should do likewise.

By the way, Sam Walton never sold any of his personal shares. This is why, long after his death, his heirs are now the wealthiest people in the world. Along the way it is fine for you to take some money "off the table," but remember, when you begin to feel a great amount of pressure, go back and read chapter eight, "Staying with Winners." Don't You Sell!

Your Mistake

Recognize that your selection of an entrepreneurial CEO may have been a mistake. Obviously, if the company you invested in fails to grow or encounters major problems, do not be afraid to take your losses and move on. As we've said before, the best investment advice ever given is to stay with the winners and sell the losers. There is no exception to this in Entrepreneurial CEO Investing.

HOW DO YOU FIND ENTREPRENEURIAL CEOS TODAY?

How do you find Entrepreneurial CEOs who meet investment criteria? It ain't easy! But it's possible, and it's worth it to make the effort.

HOW DO YOU FIND these investment-worthy entrepreneurial CEOs? It ain't easy! Since we know that one of the main investment criteria for success is whether the CEO actually owns stock in the company, how do we find these people today? At RENN Capital, we simply ask for the information because we personally meet with the managers of companies in which we invest our core holdings. Additionally, we pay about $2,000 per month for very sophisticated software that enables us to screen for entrepreneurial CEOs. But how does the individual investor obtain this information?

The good news is that the annual proxy statement filed by every public company with the SEC contains this information. The proxy statement combines information from Form 4 and Form 5, which each company files during the year. The one big trick on the proxy statement is that when you see "ownership" listed, you must look at the footnotes to tell how much is actually owned and how much is stock options. Throughout the year, any change in ownership positions must be reflected on a Form 4. Because ownership is what counts, it is very important to follow these Form 4s.

You can obtain a company's proxy statement from the SEC's website. Simply follow these easy steps:

1. Go to www.sec.gov.

2. Scroll down to the section titled "Filings & Forms (EDGAR)" and click on the "Search for Company Filings" link.

3. Scroll down to the "Historical EDGAR Archives" link and click.

4. In the box titled "EDGAR SEARCH: Enter a Search String," type in the name of the company. To the right of the "Search" button make sure the dates reflect the most recent one-year period (or cover the date range of the

proxy you are attempting to locate). Then hit the "Search" button.

5. Go to the column titled "Form Type" and scroll down until you find DEF 14A, which is your proxy statement.

6. Click on the "Text" or "HTML" link—whichever format you prefer.

7. Click on the link in the first row in the "Documents" column and this will take you to the proxy statement.

8. Go to the table of contents and locate the section titled "Security Ownership of Certain Beneficial Owners and Management" and click on that link (or scroll down to that section if there is no link).

The beneficial ownership of each director and named executive officer appear on this table. **Be certain to carefully review the footnotes so you can ascertain what portion of the beneficial ownership is actual stock and what portion is in stock options.**

ANOTHER OPTION

Another way to find ownership is by going to Bloomberg.com. Most investment brokers use this service. To use this method, your broker will follow these simple steps:

1. Type in the ticker symbol for the company.

2. Hit the "Equity" key, then PHDC.

3. Hit the "Go" key, which will give you three choices. Number three is the insiders' holdings option, which includes the CEO.

4. Hit "Three" and voilà!—you are there.

For those who want a simpler way, RENN Capital Group Inc. has launched a new service—"CEO Investing"—which lists CEOs who are significant owners, as well as other information we've deemed useful to investors. You can find information on this service at our website: www.ceoinvesting.net.

Another option is to take these principles to your stockbroker or investment adviser and tell them which companies you are interested in and ask them to help you find these companies.

As with any investment decision, it is important to do your homework. The difference here, however, is that the payoff is far greater than in traditional investing.

CEO VILLAINS

CEOs were selling hundreds of millions of dollars' worth of stocks while their companies were spiraling south.

ABOUT 95 PERCENT of the big losers in the speculative boom of 1999 and 2000 were simply investors who totally ignored the fundamentals and bought overpriced stocks where the price had nothing to do with reality. Hundreds of companies with no fundamentals to speak of—that is, no revenues and earnings—were commanding prices and market values for the whole company in the billions of dollars. Certainly this made no sense, and as a result, the losses were huge. Then, as usual, the blame game started. While there are some excesses we are going to talk about, most investors should look in the mirror and blame themselves for the stupidity they showed during this era.

Unfortunately, some top corporate management individuals took advantage of the "tulip bulb" type of boom in which we found ourselves. Many of these CEOs were selling hundreds of millions of dollars' worth of stocks while their companies were spiraling south. Over the past several years the media have written numerous articles about these corporate villains. Among them were Enron's Kenneth Lay, Tyco's Dennis Kozlowski, WorldCom's Bernie Ebbers, and Adelphia's John Rigas. Some companies, of course, survived even though the management sold huge amounts of stock, but far too many of the investors suffered losses. Overall, it is easy to see that this was a period in which corporate excesses and greed hit an all-time high.

Congress, reacting to the outcry following the market collapse of many companies and seeing the behavior of some of the senior executives, passed the Sarbanes-Oxley bill to basically reform corporate governance. Although the objectives of this bill are good, the reality is that if a company's leadership has no integrity, all the laws in the world will not protect you, the investor.

Among the best things that have happened to address these integrity issues is the reform that deals with the time period in which corporate executives must report their buying and selling. The required time frame has now been dropped from monthly reports to the filing of a report within three days of any purchases or sales. This is extremely important to investors because one of the steps in following the Entrepreneurial CEO Investing strategy is to find out who is buying and who is selling. Ironically, you could have protected yourself throughout this whole speculative boom period by simply watching what was happening with the buying and selling activities of the companies' executives. If you had been invested in one of the companies mentioned and the stock began to have large appreciations, when you began to see the CEO sell his own stock in large amounts, that would have been the clearest signal for you to get out of the stock yourself.

The truism in life holds for business as well: people generally act in their own self-interest. By having an ability to know what the chief executive is doing, you too can take appropriate action. One of the best long-term forecasters of a company's success, and therefore an indicator of an investor's ability to make money, is when management themselves buy their own shares of stock. Not options, but their own shares of stock.

During the Internet boom you saw very little personal investment by company executives, largely because the stocks were very overpriced. And, while some of the people lacked integrity, they weren't stupid. They saw Wall Street and investors bidding up their companies to totally absurd prices. But you will notice, if you look at the record, that the really dedicated CEOs came through that period of inflated prices unscathed. You didn't see Bill Gates or Warren Buffett dumping their shares in an absurd manner.

In the real world of investing, when we talk about portfolio diversification, it is because diversification can, in some ways, protect you from an occasional villain about whom you might make a mistake. It is obviously impossible to know you may have invested in a company in which the CEO falsifies the accounting or enacts other abuses that have happened. So, while you can partially protect yourself by watching what the CEO does from a buying and selling standpoint, part of your additional investment wisdom is to have a diversified portfolio. Should you end up with one or two companies in which you have made a mistake, you can still have extremely high gains if you get past the villains and stick with the dedicated CEOs.

OTHER RED FLAGS

Many of the executives who took advantage of investors during the boom did not own shares that they had purchased with their hard-earned money or sweat equity; theirs were shares they were simply given through large amounts of stock options. As a result, they thought of themselves as being in a lottery in which they had won these options, which they could turn into a quick buck by selling them.

Occasionally you will invest in companies where the management does not necessarily violate the law, but they do not act in the shareholders' best interest. One example we have personal experience with was a company called Jakks Pacific. Jack Friedman, a superb businessman who really knows the toy industry, headed up Jakks Pacific. He built the company from a $10 million business to a $600 million business in just a few years, making it one of the largest toy companies in the United States.

The big problem was that even while he was doing many good things for the company, Friedman was continually selling stock. Directors were constantly granting him new options, which he would cash in.

While investors—including our own RENN Capital Group, Inc.—did make some money if they had invested early, the success was nowhere near what it could have been, because Wall Street and the financial communities basically lost faith in Friedman. The sad reality is that if Friedman had actually kept the original stock he owned, rather than sold it, he would have become a very, very rich man and made a lot more money for not only himself but also his investors.

A recent example that upset investors in Home Depot was the departure of its CEO, Robert Nardelli, who left with $210 million after performing poorly in his job. Another similar case was the CEO of Pfizer, Hank McKinnell, who left with a huge severance package despite having disappointed the company's shareholders. Both of these gentlemen did not do anything unlawful. However, shareholders are wondering about the responsibility of each company's board of directors. (Note: Having applied the Entrepreneurial CEO Investing method, you would not have invested in either one of these companies.)

Watch for when any given CEO starts aggressively selling. You can clearly see there will be a conflict of interest if you are invested for the long term and management is constantly selling their shares. Obviously, this is a situation you would not want to be in for the long term.

LIFESTYLE MANAGEMENT VERSUS SHAREHOLDER VALUE MANAGEMENT: INVESTOR ADVICE TO THE CEO

> The idea of suddenly "winning the lottery," and giving yourself all kinds of options, is not the way to think of yourself as a partner.

WHILE THE PRIMARY FOCUS of this book is to help investors select the right entrepreneurial CEO to invest in, we thought any CEOs reading this book might benefit from a little investor advice—from our perspective.

Over the past few years CEOs have been the target of a lot of bad publicity, particularly in the aftermath of the big bear market from 2000 to 2002. There were, of course, some unsavory actions that reflected very poorly on corporate management in this country. Fortunately, this reflected on a very small minority of CEOs.

Even though Congress has enacted reforms to curtail management's abuses vis-à-vis shareholders, we maintain that you don't need the Sarbanes-Oxley bill to know what is right and what is wrong. Being an ethical CEO and treating your shareholders and employees responsibly has a great deal to do with good old common sense.

The first and easiest rule of all is to think of your shareholders as partners in the business, not as mere numbers. Warren Buffett always speaks of his shareholders as partners. The question that follows, then, is, How do you think you should treat your partners? If this question had been taken seriously, many of the unethical actions of a few bad apples would never have happened in corporate America. Shareholders are not a bunch of rustics who live in the hinterland. They are people like you who have invested in the company and deserve to be treated as partners. With this thought in mind, let's look at a number of areas that, were we CEOs, we would totally avoid.

MANAGEMENT CONTRACTS

Let's face it! Most management contracts are all one sided: everything for the executive, very little benefit for the company. If you are an owner and running the company successfully, who needs a contract? If you are a director of a public company, you need to think carefully about giving assets of the company to management without them earning it. We are all for incentives based on earnings; it is performance that must be rewarded.

Perks

Perks are really more ego trips than so-called business tools. Consider the corporate airplane. Rarely is a private corporate jet needed in business. Granted, from time to time you'll need to fly to places where airline service is very poor. But, instead of buying a plane and maintaining an expensive staff, be realistic. You can charter planes. Admittedly, this is somewhat costly, but it is nowhere near as costly as owning and maintaining a private corporate jet or turboprop. Today there are also new options such as time-sharing, which can dramatically reduce the cost of private plane use. Yet the fact remains: you can get to most places without a private plane, so there's little need for one.

Another area of contention is travel itself. In all our years of traveling over millions of miles, none of us has ever once purchased a first-class ticket. Why? We have a rule here at RENN Capital Group, Inc.: we all fly coach unless we're flying overseas. Even then, we fly only business class. Because of the collective mileage flown, we have been able to upgrade to first class, but we've never bought first-class tickets. We think you set a much better example for all your employees if you fly just like they are expected to. Therefore, never buy a first-class ticket.

Salaries

As part owners of the business, the CEO and the management team should either have shares in the company or options by way of reward and show of appreciation. The idea that there is all carrot and no stick has been one of the most distressing trends in corporate America. Nobody begrudges a CEO making a good salary, but taking absurd monies based on some kind of so-called analysis of what other CEOs are making is one of the great abuses in companies today. This practice needs to end. Along with fair salaries, nobody begrudges a CEO having an incentive plan based on making money for the shareholders. However, many incentive plans are based on top-line or other performances, which have very little to do with achieving true financial results for the shareholders.

The other major area of abuse has come from giving excessive stock options to CEOs. A major force afoot in the accounting industry says stock options need to be accounted for, just like giving shares, as an expense of the company. Stock options as well as giving shares in the company can be effective employee incentives, but the reasonableness test needs to be applied. The idea of suddenly "winning the lottery," and giving yourself all kinds of options, is not the way to think of yourself as a partner.

Other perks for CEOs include cars, country club memberships, purchased artwork, etc. About 90 percent of these gifts should be eliminated. If you want to buy artwork, don't put it on the shareholders' backs; make the purchase with your own money. Ask yourself, Would Warren Buffett ever buy a $6,000 shower curtain à la the former Tyco chairman's extravagance?

SELLING OUT

One of the most important areas to examine is whether CEOs are constantly selling their own shares. There is probably no better test of the CEO's true motives than whether he is more interested in selling shares and decreasing his interest in the company than in keeping his stock and being a major owner. We talked about this in earlier chapters. We don't believe any investor should object to a CEO's occasional sale of stock to create some diversification, to build a new house, to start a family foundation, etc. But don't lie to the shareholders when they know you are selling your shares—for purely selfish reasons.

PUTTING ON AIRS

The best CEOs, it seems, never act like big shots. Ownership is respected. One of the great premises of Entrepreneurial CEO Investing is that when people own a major part of the company, they don't have to try to create something that's not in the best interest of shareholders, because they, themselves, are the biggest shareholders. While most really successful CEOs are thinking of building an estate and creating wealth, they don't flaunt their success to others.

Not so amazingly, the CEO who thinks of himself as a fiduciary for and a partner with his shareholders—instead of constantly trying to enrich himself—usually ends up being the richest of them all. That, of course, is one of the great principles of Entrepreneurial CEO Investing: finding the Bill Gateses and the Sam Waltons and others who have created huge long-term value for their shareholders while also creating tremendous value for themselves. When this happens success happens, and it epitomizes the very best form of leading from any CEO.

FOUR TO WATCH

Today's greatest opportunities lie in the emerging businesses led by the types of entrepreneurial CEOs who have led before them. How do you find them? The search is on.

TO HELP GET YOU STARTED on your journey of Entrepreneurial CEO Investing, here are four CEOs of emerging companies whom we believe have met all the criteria we've outlined. They also think globally. Let these be your guide as you begin to do your own research and build your own Entrepreneurial CEO Investing portfolio.

Google, Inc.
(NASDAQ: GOOG)

Google is the best near-term example of what entrepreneurship can do in a short time. Only a few years ago Google was merely in the minds of two young men—Larry Page and Sergey Brim. They were graduate students together at Stanford University, both thinking they would have academic careers similar to their parents'. Along the way they found a radical new approach to Internet searches—a search engine technology that could provide a "gold mine" of information. They also redefined how to be paid for this service, something that had escaped many of the earlier Internet companies.

Each of the two founders currently holds 36.4 million shares of Google stock, placing them in the very enviable position of being among the wealthiest of all Americans. While Page and Brim remain the driving force behind Google, they have also built a strong team, beginning with hiring Eric Schmidt as the CEO. Schmidt is also a major owner in Google, with 13.9 million shares. Of the class A and B common stocks, the executive officers and directors own a whopping 76.7 percent of the company, according to the last proxy statement. This is entrepreneurship at its highest.

Google stock only became public in 2004 in a unique auction. The price was $84 per share. In 2006, shares have sold for as high as $475 per share. If you had invested $10,000 in the initial offering, your investment would, in a year and a half, be worth $56,547. That's not a bad start.

It remains to be seen whether this "money machine" can keep growing. The management says Google has just graduated from "grade school." The market capitalization is currently about $125 billion, so there is market risk. Nevertheless, at Google we do have all the makings of an entrepreneurial CEO mega-stock.

WHOLE FOODS MARKET, INC.
(NASDAQ: WFMI)

Over the past decade enormous attention has been paid to health and well-being. One school of thought for a way to live a healthy, long life has been directed toward eating naturally grown organic foods, along with taking nutritional supplements. Right in the "fairway" of this trend is Whole Foods Market, based in Austin, Texas, which owns and operates a chain of natural food supermarkets throughout the United States. The company has grown rapidly and is now a multibillion-dollar business, but its focus still seems to be in its infancy.

The driving force behind Whole Foods Market is John P. Mackey, chairman and CEO. He currently owns 1.2 million shares. While not a large percent of the company, his ownership is significant and has made him a very wealthy man.

Whole Foods Market went public in 1992 at an adjusted price of $2.15 per share. A $10,000 investment at the offering price would have resulted in 4,700 shares. At the current price of $46 per share, the value of that $10,000 investment would be $216,200, or nearly twenty-two times your money. This company is a classic example of how a strong leader with a clear vision can create value by being in a business that is doing good in the world.

OmniVision Technologies, Inc.
(NASDAQ: OVTI)

OmniVision Technologies provides integrated single-chip semi-conductor imaging devices. The company develops and markets these imaging devices for computer, communications, and consumer electronics applications. These "tiny little optics" products are currently being used in cameras, cell phones, personal computers, and digital and security cameras. There seems to be no end to the potential uses of these devices.

Two Chinese-American men, Shaw Hong and He Xinping, founded OmniVision. They met while working together at Motorola for a number of years. Later on, Raymond Wu, another American-born Chinese businessman, joined them.

These engineers have been able to do what no other group was able to accomplish: they placed a tiny lens on a semiconductor chip. This marriage enabled cell phone makers to put a low-cost camera in the unit.

Shaw Hong, the company's current CEO, owns beneficially 1,568,000 shares and has options on another 318,000 shares. Under his leadership OmniVision has grown rapidly. Its market capitalization is now at $1.4 billion.

OmniVision went public in July 2000, at $6.50 per share, adjusting for stock splits. The stock has been as high as $35 per share.

We think this company has the makings of a mega-stock, with its strong entrepreneurial CEO who has a clear vision for the future. In fact, OVTI is currently held in one of the funds managed by RENN Capital Group, Inc.

Comtech, Inc.
(NASDAQ: COGO)

Comtech, Inc., is incorporated in the United States, but its main operating businesses are in China. The company provides specialized design solutions and services to the two hundred largest technical companies in China. Important areas include telecom, mobile devices, and consumer electronics manufacturers in China. Continuing revenue services include a joint venture with China Telecom for locating the position of cell phones. The first service is aimed at children's cell phones.

Comtech has been growing rapidly, with more than $100 million in revenues and a current market capitalization of $330 million. Profitability and margins are quite high due to the service nature of the business. The company has the classic signs of the entrepreneurial CEO. Jeffrey Kang began this company about seven years ago with a personal $50,000 investment. He currently owns approximately 50 percent of the common stock. Kang's vision is to build a major specialized technology company in China. Similar to other successful entrepreneurial CEOs, he has hired an excellent management team.

Comtech went public in October 2004 through a reverse merger of a publicly traded U.S. company. A private placement was complete at $3.50 per share, which represented the price of the trading shares at that time. A $10,000 investment in the fall of 2004 would have bought you 2,857 shares. Currently, they have been trading at $18.50 per share. In a little more than two years your $10,000 investment would have grown to $52,854— an impressive gain of 429 percent.

Comtech is directly playing on the technology growth of China, but the real driving force is the entrepreneurship of Jeffrey Kang and his team. If the Entrepreneurial CEO Investing philosophy is correct, you should be able to "ride" this investment for a long time. (RENN Capital Group, Inc. managed funds have a major holding in this stock, with more than 1.3 million shares.)

CEO INVESTING WORDWIDE

These same criteria for Entrepreneurial CEO Investing in the United States can also be applied worldwide. You will find that mega-gains are occurring in Great Britain, Europe, China, Korea, Japan, and India through the application of this concept. The selection problem is more difficult in some areas, however, because the reporting requirements that U.S. companies are subject to are not required in some of these other countries. But make no mistake about it; entrepreneurs are driving world economic growth. This is why China is growing at three times the rate of the United States.

It is not the Chinese government that has created the wealth in China. It is entrepreneurship set free! Fortunately, there's a direct way for investors in the United States to participate in the entrepreneurial CEO growth in China. Certain Chinese firms have incorporated in the United States and have either a public offering or a reverse merger (taking an existing U.S. publicly traded company and merging). This allows U.S. investors to buy shares in those select Chinese companies. The benefit to U.S. investors is to be able to join successful Chinese CEOs and become long-term shareholders.

In this process U.S. investors are protected in the following ways:

- U.S. security laws, including Sarbanes-Oxley, are applied
- General Accepted Accounting Principles (GAAP) are honored
- The companies are listed on and supervised by NASDAQ, the American Stock Exchange, or the New York Stock Exchange

A number of these types of companies are in the current RENN Capital Group, Inc. managed funds, including Comtech, Inc., as we mentioned earlier.

In today's global economy it makes good sense to consider worldwide options of Entrepreneurial CEO Investing.

PART II:

CASE STUDIES OF ENTREPRENEURIAL CEOs

We have selected ten case studies to illustrate Entrepreneurial CEO Investing. You will notice they cross many different industry lines. Each one would have met the CEO investing principles and scored high on the CEO Checklist. Reading about and understanding these CEOs will give you good examples of what to look for in your own investment portfolio. Pay particular attention to each one's vision and leadership.

WOULD YOU LIKE TO SWING ON A STAR?: WARREN BUFFETT

Not only is Warren Buffett considered the most successful investor of the twentieth and twenty-first centuries, but he also is considered by many to be the greatest investor of all time. Berkshire Hathaway, Inc., (NYSE: BRK/A), was trading in the public market at $20 per share when Warren Buffett assumed control. Because he doesn't believe in stock splits or dividends the stock has never been split, with only 2 million shares outstanding. In January 2007, the shares traded at $108,850 per share. No, that's no typo; that's the correct amount.

If you had been an original investor in 1965, your $10,000 investment would have given you 500 shares. At today's value, those shares would be worth $54,425,000.

AMONG THE BEST-KNOWN ENTREPRENEURIAL CEOs in the world today is Warren Buffett. He is the poster child for Entrepreneurial CEO Investing. He fits all the criteria, and he's amassed his own fortune by investing in a similar manner. Not only is Buffett considered the most successful investor of the twentieth and twenty-first centuries, but he also is considered by many to be the greatest investor of all time. Investors read his annual report messages as if they were the Bible, hoping to glean a nugget of truth they can use for themselves. And, if you attend the annual meeting in Omaha, Nebraska, you can get a free ice cream cone at the local Dairy Queen.

As chairman of Berkshire Hathaway, Buffett is the owner of arguably the most successful publicly traded company primarily due to his stock-picking abilities—a talent that has made both him and his investors very wealthy people. The stock has never been split, with only 2 million shares outstanding. Buffett doesn't believe in stock splits or paying dividends. When he took over Berkshire Hathaway, the shares were trading at $20 per share. As of January 2007, shares traded at $108,850 per share. Yes, that's right. Buffett's salary is less than the price of one share!

Buffett still owns 502,964 shares (or 32 percent) of the company's stock, making him one of the wealthiest men in the world.

The second of three children, Buffett was the only son of a stockbroker-turned–Republican congressman. It is said that Buffett displayed an amazing aptitude early on for both money and business. He would impress his friends by memorizing the population of numerous U.S. cities, and by age eleven, he was marking the board at his father's brokerage firm. At that same age Buffett bought his first stock: three shares of Cities Service Preferred, at $38 a share. When the price dropped to $27, young Buffett held tight, and when it recovered to $40, he sold, making a $6 profit. Unfortunately, he missed a far bigger profit because the company's stock subsequently rose to $200 a share. This became young Warren's first lesson in patience.

In 1947, at the age of seventeen, when Buffett graduated from high school, he had already saved $5,000 delivering news-papers. (That sum was equal to more than $43,000 in 2004.) Four years later, as a senior at the University of Nebraska, Buffett truly caught the investment bug. He read a book titled *The Intelligent Investor*, written by Benjamin Graham, who advised investors to ignore the trends that sweep Wall Street and instead search for stocks that trade well below their actual value. Graham called these stocks "cigar butts"—companies the stock market dis-carded but that still had a few "puffs" of value left. While the search for such companies required tremendous patience and analysis, the challenge appealed to Buffett and his mathemati-cal skills. When Buffett was rejected by Harvard Business School, he moved to New York and began to study with Graham at Columbia University. There, Buffett earned a masters in eco-nomics and began working for his mentor.

In 1957, feeling somewhat constrained by Graham's rigid rules of investing, Buffett began to question whether it would make as much sense to buy good businesses at a fair price as dying businesses at a cheap price. He returned to his hometown of Omaha, Nebraska, and began his first investment partnership.

A group of local investors put in $25,000 each, and Buffett put in $100,000 of his own money. He appointed himself general partner and started to purchase stocks. His goal was to beat the Dow Jones by an average of 10 percent a year. Twelve years later, when the partnership dissolved, Buffett's investment had exploded at a compound rate of 29.5 percent versus a mere 7.4 percent for the Dow.

One of the struggling company stocks that Buffett had purchased in 1962 was a textile mill called Berkshire Hathaway. As the U.S. textile industry dried up in the face of foreign competition, Buffett had the foresight to reallocate the company's capital into a variety of other businesses, including insurance. That turned out to be a classic move. Because of the "float" of cash within the insurance industry, soon Berkshire was generating millions of dollars. As if luck was with him, the insurance-generated cash came along just as the financial markets went into their largest drop since the 1930s. Buffett, who had become very savvy at spotting values, filled his portfolio with viable companies whose stock began to rise once the market regained its momentum.

At the time of this writing, Buffett owns a 32 percent stake in Berkshire Hathaway, giving him a net worth of more than $36 billion, making him the second wealthiest man in the world, just behind his friend Bill Gates. Yet, if you think he lives lavishly, think again. As chairman and CEO his annual salary is a mere $100,000. He still lives on Farnam Street in Omaha, in the same gray stucco house he purchased some forty years ago for $31,500. He's said to eat hamburgers or steaks for lunch and dinner, drinking Coca-Cola with every meal. (Note: Buffett first invested in Coca-Cola in 1988, at a time when Wall Street saw little value in the $10.96 a share stock. Today Buffett is on the board of directors of the soft drink company.) His one streak of extravagance is his Gulfstream IV-SP jet, which he fondly calls "The Indefensible."

In 2006, Buffett announced that most of his fortune would go to the Bill and Melinda Gates Foundation to help make the world a little better.

CASE STUDY 2

NOW COMPUTE THIS: MICHAEL DELL

One of the greatest entrepreneurial CEOs of the past twenty years is Michael Dell. Like many other successful entrepreneurs, Dell got his start early. In his case, he sold computer parts from his college dorm room. But being a trend in the industry wasn't the thrust of his success. Over the past decade, the computer equipment industry has been a complex "minefield" with few competitors having the tenacity or business savvy to continute to exist. Dell, however, has prospered, making multi-millions for many.

DELL HAS BECOME ONE OF THE WEALTHIEST MEN in America; yet, as a young man, he still has much in front of him left to accomplish.

Dell, Inc. (NASDAQ: DELL), went public in June 1988 at an adjusted price of $0.09 per share. A $10,000 investment at that time would now equal 111,111 shares. At the current price of $26.25 per share, that would equate to $2,917,000. Each dollar invested would have multiplied 291 times. Now that's something to compute!

If Michael Dell had not followed his natural talents and interests, instead of reading about him as the founder of one of *Fortune* magazine's most admired companies, you may never have heard of him. Unless, that is, you needed medical services. Yes, when Michael Dell entered college he intended to become a doctor. But his true love was working with computers—a love that won out.

Not unlike his role model, Sam Walton, Dell was not about to let lack of money deter his quest for venturing into a dream he believed in. With little money at all, Dell began conducting business out of his University of Texas dorm room in 1983. According to him, being an entrepreneur wasn't something he consciously set out to do. Instead, it was vision, innovation, tenacity, and a willingness to take a risk that was compelling to Dell.

At a time when other computer makers were marketing to the general consumer through traditional retail outlets, Dell had an idea to sell computers to consumers directly and to design these computers based upon the customers' own specifications, not what Dell thought they needed. So, one year after he started selling custom-made PCs and components from his dorm room, Dell officially set up his business with a mere $1,000 in capital. The rest, as they say, is history.

It is Dell's innovative thinking, strong work ethic, and willingness to take risks that have enabled his company to enjoy phenomenal growth and profitability. The importance of having a clear strategy continues to be one of Dell's greatest strengths. Dell has been quoted as recognizing that within a company of more than forty thousand employees, his ability to impact anything but strategy is "pretty small." Dell admits, "Strategy is the biggest point of impact I can have." It is that strategy—that innovative thinking that enabled Dell to launch his unique concept more than twenty years ago—that serves him so well in continuing to create tremendous value for Dell's customers, employees, and shareholders. In 2007, Dell, after relinquishing the CEO job in 2004, has returned to his original position after unfavorable results. The entrepreneur is back!

SOFTWARE SAVVY: BILL GATES

Microsoft is one of the gold standards for Entrepreneurial CEO Investing.

It is difficult to believe that Microsoft has only been public since March 1986. The stock originally went public at $21 per share. Adjusted for stock splits, that cost basis would be 7 cents today. An initial $10,000 investment would, as of January 2007, be 142,857 shares. At the January 2007 price of $29.80 per share (NASDAQ: MSFT), that $10,000 initial investment would be worth $4,257,000.

ACCORDING TO *FORBES* MAGAZINE, Bill Gates is the wealthiest man in the world, with an estimated worth of $53.0 billion in 2006. Not bad for a Harvard dropout.

Gates was born and grew up in Seattle, Washington, the son of an attorney father and a teacher mother. He and his two sisters had a comfortable childhood, with Gates attending public school until the seventh grade, when he entered Seattle's exclusive Lakeside School. There he met Paul Allen, who shared Gates's interest in computers. They became good friends, and in 1972 the two founded Traf-O-Data, a company that designed and built computerized car-counting machines for traffic analysis.

Three years later, while they were attending Harvard, they developed a version of the BASIC programming language for an Albuquerque, New Mexico, computer company named MITS. This became the start of their microcomputer software business. Gates recognized that in order to devote appropriate time to the business, he would have to drop out of college. So, in his junior year, he did just that, with a plan to "take time off" and return to Harvard. He never did. Instead, in the summer of 1975, when Gates was just nineteen years old, he and Paul Allen incorporated their little company named Microsoft.

Paul Allen left Microsoft eight years later, in 1983, but he has remained on the company's board of directors. Gates has provided both the business and technical leadership ever since. His foresight and vision for personal computing have been central to Microsoft's success and the success of the software industry in general. Under his leadership the company's mission has been to continually advance and improve software technology and to demonstrate that long-term commitment. Approximately $6.2 billion has been allocated for research and development for the 2005 fiscal year.

In 1994 Bill Gates married Melinda French, a business manager at Microsoft. They have three children and have been highly committed to philanthropy. Together they have endowed the Bill and Melinda Gates Foundation with more than $33 billion (as of January 2007) to support philanthropic initiatives in the areas of global health and learning.

Although Gates continues to play an active role in Microsoft as chairman of the board and chief software architect, he named longtime friend Steve Ballmer as the corporation's CEO. Gates owns 9.8 percent of the company. Along the way, he has made many others very wealthy, including his original partner, Paul Allen, whom *Forbes* names as the fifth richest man in the world, with an estimated worth of $16 billion. Many employees became multimillionaires as well, including Ballmer, whom *Forbes* lists as the nineteenth richest man in the world, with an estimated worth of $13.6 billion in 2007.

ZONED FOR SUCCESS:
J. R. HYDE III

If as an investor in 1991 you had said, "Hey, I think I'll invest in a retail auto parts chain," most Wall Street brokers would likely have suggested you visit a psychologist. Of course, they did not know J. R. Hyde III, the entrepreneurial CEO and founder of AutoZone, Inc. (NYSE: AZO), nor just what he had in mind.

Today, AutoZone is a multibillion-dollar company, and its investors have been rewarded handsomely.

The company went public in April 1991 at $5.75 per share. As of 2007, the stock had soared to $120 per share. A $10,000 investment in 1991 would have given you 1,729 shares by 2007, valued at $207,000. Most would agree that after fourteen years, making twenty times your initial investment for such a mundane industry is not too bad!

A CAN-DO, ENTREPRENEURIAL SPIRIT was nothing new to J. R. (Pitt) Hyde III. He grew up surrounded by entrepreneurs and credits much of his success to that exposure. Hyde's father and grandfather both built businesses from the ground up, providing an inspiration for the third-generation Hyde to do the same.

Hyde earned a bachelor's degree in economics from the University of North Carolina in 1965 and later joined the company founded by his grandfather in 1907—Malone & Hyde, Inc. At the wholesale food company he initiated and developed a specialty retailing division, starting with drugstores and later expanding with sporting goods stores, supermarkets, and auto parts stores. In 1972 Hyde assumed the role of chairman, making him the youngest chairman of any company listed on the New York Stock Exchange. Under his leadership the company had dramatic growth, becoming the nation's third largest wholesale food distributor in the country, with annual sales of more than $3 billion.

In 1979 Hyde founded Auto Shack, an auto parts store, in Forrest City, Arkansas, as a division of Malone & Hyde. By 1984 the division had become the first auto parts retailer to create a quality control program for its parts, demonstrating its commitment to quality and service. A year later the company adopted the motto "What it takes to do the job right." The slogan reflected the company's commitment to giving customers, the first time they asked, the parts and service they needed to do the job right—a commitment still in effect today.

Much of the success of the service philosophy ingrained in the auto parts stores can be attributed to Hyde's forefathers' entrepreneurial mind-set. When the Society of Entrepreneurs honored Hyde in 1992, he reflected: "I grew up watching both my grandfather and my father build businesses from the ground up. They took risks that many people considered unwise, and they succeeded, despite the odds. I believe my exposure to this type of 'pioneering' mind-set from a very young age gave me the drive to try new, unproven ventures. When I start a new venture, I always remember my father's statement: 'No individual ever builds a business. The individual builds an organization, and the organization builds the business.'"

Hyde's mentors taught him well. In 1987 he took a risk and spun off Auto Shack from Malone & Hyde, making it a freestanding company. The company was renamed AutoZone, and Hyde served as its first chairman and CEO. During that same year the retailer introduced WITT-JR, the first electronic catalog in the industry, used for looking up parts for vehicles and keeping up with warranty information. The concept helps AutoZone provide better, quicker service to its customers.

In 1991 AutoZone made its debut on the New York Stock Exchange at $5.75 per share. That same year it became the first auto parts retailer to register customer warranties in a computer database—still the only auto parts retailer to offer this service. Four years later, AutoZone had opened its thousandth store. The company also introduced a new Duralast battery and a Duralast Gold battery—the best-selling automotive battery in America today. In 1996 AutoZone acquired ALLDATA, a software company that provides automotive diagnostic and repair information.

With unprecedented growth under Hyde's direction, AutoZone continued to grow. By 1997, when Hyde retired from active management, the company had sales of $2.7 billion, with a net income of $195 million, and was serving customers in more than fifteen hundred stores in twenty-nine states. Today Hyde is owner and president of Pittco Holdings, Inc., a private institutional investment company.

J. R. Hyde III's entrepreneurial philosophy has served both him and his shareholders well. Today AutoZone is the nation's leading auto parts chain, with more than twenty-eight hundred stores in forty states, plus eleven in Mexico. Additionally, AutoZone sells heavy-duty truck parts through TruckPro stores; automotive diagnostic and repair software through ALLDATA; and diagnostic and repair information through alldatadiy.com. As of 2007, AutoZone shares sold at $120 per share. A $10,000 investment made in 1991 would by 2007 have given you 1,739 shares, worth $207,000. Making twenty times your investment in such a mundane industry is not too bad.

Entrepreneurial risk was not the only thing ingrained in Hyde. His grandfather and father also taught him about the responsibility of investing in one's community through charitable and civic support, which goes hand in hand with financial success. Hyde has contributed greatly to the city of Memphis, where he lives with his wife, Barbara. He is heavily involved in such organizations as the Memphis Biotech Foundation, National Civil

Rights Museum, and Greater Memphis Arts Council. The Hyde Family Foundation has generously provided extensive funds to these and numerous other organizations.

Although Hyde is no longer involved in AutoZone's day-to-day activities, he remains on its board of directors. He also serves on other corporate boards, including FedEx Corporation.

LOW-FARE HIGH FLYER: HERB KELLEHER

Southwest's (NYSE: LUV) initial public offering was in June 1971. Adjusted for splits, the cost basis per share would be $0.10. A $10,000 investment would now give the investor 100,000 shares. At the January 2007 depressed price of $16 per share, that would still equate to $1,600,000. According to an airline analyst, Southwest's stock was recently selling for more than all other U.S. airlines combined. Now, that's a high flyer!

HE'S BEEN CALLED "zany, down-to-earth, crazy," and "nuts," but both Wall Street brokers and Southwest Airlines customers agree that his wacky tactics work for investors and airline passengers alike.

HERB KELLEHER was the lawyer for businessman Rollin King, who had an idea for a new type of airline—one that could fly passengers quickly across short distances, and do it cheaply. The idea was considered outlandish by traditionalists, but despite naysayers, King and Kelleher decided to give the idea a shot.

At its inception, Southwest did not cross state borders. Instead, it flew exclusively within the state of Texas, which meant it did not have to follow the ticket prices mandated by the Civil Aeronautics Board. This enabled the airline to dramatically reduce fares, making the airline an instant hit with passengers. The airline's early success did not settle well with its competitors, however, who readily recognized Southwest's potential. Southwest's arrival was fought through litigation by Braniff, Continental, and Texas International, but without success. It was Herb Kelleher who argued the airline's case and won. Thus, Southwest Airlines made its maiden voyage in 1971 with service between Dallas, Houston, and San Antonio.

Talk about starting small—Southwest began with four planes and fewer than seventy employees. Early on, when the company was faced with financial issues, Kelleher and his partner were forced to make a choice: sell one of its planes or lay off some of its employees. They made a very unconventional choice—they sold the plane. In return, their employees were asked to cut gate turnaround time to fifteen minutes. Remarkably, the employees agreed. This marked the beginning of one of the friendliest management-labor relationships in the airline industry—a relationship that has endured through all these years. It also marked the line in the sand for the type of culture that would exist in a company run by Kelleher. His zany personality and his philosophy about keeping a fun-filled culture have long endeared him to the airline's employees. Kelleher says he simply hires the best people, treats them with respect, and gives them the freedom to make decisions and to have fun just being themselves. It's a philosophy that has created what some may consider an offbeat culture, albeit a successful one.

Kelleher has likewise become known among business associates for his nontraditional way of confronting issues. Take, for example, his uncanny way of settling an advertising dispute with the CEO of Stevens Aviation. Both Stevens and Southwest were using the advertising tagline "Plane Smart." To settle the dispute, Kelleher had an outrageous suggestion: he and Stevens's CEO would have an arm-wrestling match, with the winner retaining the rights to the slogan. Although Kelleher lost the match, the competition garnered so much goodwill and publicity that Stevens allowed Southwest to continue to use the tagline.

Southwest was the first airline to develop a frequent flyer program, giving credit to passengers for the number of trips taken rather than just the number of miles flown. They also pioneered senior discounts, Fun Fares, Fun Packs, a same-day air-freight delivery service, and ticketless travel, among other unique programs. They have consistently earned the highest customer service ratings in the airline industry and have incurred the lowest number of complaints per one hundred thousand customers of any airline. Furthermore, Southwest has one of the lowest employee turnover rates, at 4.5 percent, and has been a frequent top ten company in *Fortune* magazine's "Best Companies to Work

For" list. And Condé Nast's *Traveler* magazine named Southwest "the safest airline in the world." All that and profitable, too? Not bad for a zany man and his equally zany ideas!

Kelleher stepped down from his day-to-day responsibilities on June 19, 2001, but he continues to serve on Southwest's board of directors. In the years since Rollin King and Herb Kelleher began Southwest, the airline has grown from being a regional upstart to being the nation's fifth largest airline. That makes Southwest Airlines a great company to invest in—even in an era of inflated fuel prices and market uncertainties.

CLEAR SKIES WITH CLEAR CHANNEL: LOWRY MAYS

Lowry Mays and his Clear Channel Communications, Inc. (NYSE: CCU), are a soaring example of what a leader's vision can do for investors.

When it came to radio, television, and billboards, Lowry Mays refused to fall in love with the media. Instead, he saw the entities as pure "advertising vehicles." The results for investors have been nothing but blue skies. Clear Channel's initial public offering was in April 1981 at an adjusted price of $0.32. A $10,000 investment at that time would be the equivalent today of 31,250 shares. At the stock's buyout price of $37.60 (the company's sale will be completed in 2007), that would give the investor a tidy sum of $1,175,000.

Now that's a baby-blue clear-sky investment.

L□□RY MAYS is the poster child for proving that it's not the industry an investor should be overly concerned about, it's the vision and leadership at the helm of the business that really counts.

Mays's primary role was that of an investment banker until 1972, when one of his clients backed out of a deal to buy an FM radio station in San Antonio, Texas. Despite his lack of experience in that industry, Mays nevertheless had a clear vision for developing a profitable venture. Along with his partner B. J. McCombs, Mays bought the radio station and formed San Antonio Broadcasting Company. That purchase was not for love of music or programming, but to sell advertising. In 1975 Mays acquired AM station WOAI, the company's first "Clear Channel" radio station, which was designated with its own frequency nationwide.

Mays's concept to grow profits through advertising proved to be highly profitable. After acquiring Broad Street Communications Company in 1984, Clear Channel made its initial public offering on the NASDAQ. Four years later they entered the television business with the acquisition of WPMI-TV, and in 1989, they created Clear Channel Sports, which owns the radio rights to certain NCAA sports events. In 1994 Mays obtained listing of Clear Channel Communications, Inc., Common Stock.

By the end of 1996 Clear Channel owned 101 radio stations in the United States, with $352 million in revenue. Three years later it owned 557 stations and 555,000 billboards, with $2.7 billion in sales. The *Wall Street Journal* ranked the company as the fifth best-performing stock of the 1990s.

Clearly, the advertising synergy concept was a winning idea. The company's billboards promote the company's radio stations, which promote its concert tours, which are managed by the company's in-house promotions firm and are played at company-owned or company-operated venues. Clear Channel is everywhere.

At the end of 2003, Clear Channel controlled 1,182 radio stations, 788,000 billboards, and 103 entertainment venues in the United States, and its event-promotion business sold more tickets in the first half of that year than all its closest forty-nine competitors combined. By 2004 the company had $9 billion in annual sales and a market value of $29 billion.

The larger-than-life Lowry Mays was born in Houston, the oldest of two children, and raised in Dallas. His mother was a real estate agent and his father was a steel company executive who died when Lowry was twelve. The 6-foot 2-inch youth graduated from Texas A&M University with a degree in petroleum engineering and later earned an MBA from Harvard before entering the profession of investment banking. Through the years many have credited Mays's folksy, backslapping, laid-back Texas style for his success in buying up struggling companies and adding them to Clear Channel's media mix.

Mays also took time to groom his two sons, Mark and Randall, to run the business someday. Mark joined the company in 1989 and Randall in 1992. Today Randall has settled into the role of chief financial officer, while Mark has become the heir apparent. The time for Mays's sons to assume their leading roles came earlier than planned and in an unwanted way, however.

On the morning of April 30, 2004, Lowry Mays awoke with a numbing sensation and was rushed to the hospital. He had been stricken with a blood clot in his brain, which required immediate surgery. Mays was paralyzed by the stroke, but in the fall of 2004, he surprised company directors when he rolled his wheelchair into a board meeting.

That incident reminded Mark and Randall of a comment their father made once when they had driven by the Oklahoma City headquarters of the Oklahoma Publishing Company founded by Edward King Gaylord. Gaylord went to work every day until his death in 1974. Lowry is said to have pointed to the building and told his sons, "That's where Eddie Gaylord died at his desk at the age of 101. I should be so lucky." The company is now being acquired and will be private.

YOUR AMERICAN DREAM: ANGELO MOZILO

One of the themes of this book is the reality that you can have mega-stock gains even when you invest in an ordinary business, as long as that business has extraordinary leadership. No stock represents achieving this American dream more clearly than the story of Countrywide Financial Corporation (NYSE: CFC) and Angelo Mozilo.

Countrywide's business was created around home mortgage loans, and its concept quickly spread across the country. Countrywide went public in 1969 at an adjusted price of $0.14. Your initial $10,000 investment would currently give you 71,428 shares. Trading at the recent price of $42 per share would equal $3,000,000. If you had invested in Countrywide's initial offering, by January 2007 you would have made three hundred times your initial investment—enough to make anyone's American dream come true.

WORK DILIGENTLY toward helping others get what they want and you will be rewarded as well. Sounds like a nice philosophy, but can it really work? Just ask Angelo Mozilo and David Loeb, cofounders of Countrywide Home Loans. That's exactly the philosophy that is embodied in the most successful home mortgage company in the country today.

The son of a butcher, Angelo Mozilo graduated from Fordham University in 1960 and entered the mortgage banking industry. Nine years later he cofounded Countrywide with $500,000 and three employees. From the very beginning he played the role of chief salesman, leaving much of the numbers duties to others. And from the very beginning he was compelled to help those less fortunate. For example, when he would present home loan applications to the Veterans Administration on behalf of his clients, bureaucracy would often get in the way, and officials would routinely turn veteran applicants down. "I'd tell the rejected veterans to bring their medals, canes, and artificial limbs and sit in the VA office," Mozilo told *Fortune* magazine in an interview. "Then I'd go down and yell at the bureaucrats, 'These people spilled blood for their country! This is a disgrace!'" The result? He got almost every application approved.

To this day, Mozilo has never veered from his original mission to lower the cost of home ownership, to educate consumers about the process of owning a home, and to remove the barriers to ownership.

Countrywide was one of America's first lenders to offer a low down-payment home loan, which was a tremendous help to low-to-moderate income borrowers. In 1998 the company's "We

House America" program set a primary goal of assisting 570,000 low-income and minority consumers by funding $50 billion in home loans. One year later, that goal was increased to $80 billion, increasing the number of individuals who could benefit from the funding to an estimated 800,000 people nationwide.

Among the strategies used then and now to fulfill Mozilo's mission are the following:

- Countrywide expanded partnerships with nonprofit and community-based organizations that seek to increase home ownership

- The company supports housing initiatives that benefit lower-income and minority families

- A diverse workforce is employed, attracting dedicated individuals who are members of the very communities they serve

- An active outreach program makes them an active participant in home buying fairs, seminars, and a variety of programs that enable Countrywide to spread the message that home ownership is an attainable goal

- Countrywide offers a vast selection of information, tools, and educational resources that help customers receive financial loans and understand their rights as consumers

Today, Countrywide originates home loans, provides servicing, trades mortgage-backed securities, sells title insurance, and operates a bank funded by the billions in property tax and insurance payments the company holds in escrow for its customers.

It is the only independent left in an industry now dominated by major banks. Countrywide ranks as the second largest home-loan provider in America, ahead of Washington Mutual and right after Wells Fargo. Amazingly, the company has generated the best stock market performance of any financial services company in the Fortune 500 over the past two decades.

As long as Mozilo remains an integral force at Countrywide, it is unlikely there will be any change in the basic philosophies that have made the company the success that it is. Mozilo explained his philosophies this way in a conversation for the *Graziadio Business Report*: "If you look at companies that are over one hundred years old, you will find that they have one thing in common; their primary focus is not the bottom line. They are dedicated to making a difference in people's lives. It is very clear to me that a company will have a very short shelf life if leadership is focused solely on the bottom line. There is a long history of companies where the innovators, or the entrepreneurs, leave the company and new management enters the picture and immediately sets out to improve the bottom line. They will cut costs, cut personnel and cut quality." Mozilo's objective is to make sure that never happens at Countrywide—at least not as long as he is there.

MAKE MINE A GRANDE:
HOWARD SCHULTZ

Who would have "thunk it"—people paying $2.50 for a cup of coffee and standing in line for the privilege. Today, the demand is no longer just in America, but around the world.

The visionary behind the Starbucks Corporation (NAS-DAQ: SBUX) is Howard Schultz, a poor boy from the Bronx.

A relative newcomer to the stock market, Starbucks went public in June 1992 at an adjusted price of $1.06 per share. A $10,000 investment at that time would now equate to 9,434 shares. At the recent price of $35.50 per share, the value of that initial investment would be $335,000. Making thirty-four times your initial investment in just twelve years will pay for a lot of grande lattes, and it appears this unique retail chain has a lot of new caffeine addicts yet to conquer around the world.

CONSIDER THIS: How serious would you have been about investing in a company whose chairman and chief strategist believed that the marketing of a $3 latte was a recession-proof business? Well, if you had had the vision and courage to believe in Howard Schultz and his gutsy thinking, you too could be wealthy.

Schultz wasn't the founder of the incredibly successful Starbucks concept. As a matter of fact, he wasn't even educated or experienced in the business of roasted coffee. But he was a visionary who had the ability to spot potential.

Schultz was a vice president for a manufacturer of stylish kitchen equipment and housewares. In this capacity he spotted a small company in the state of Washington that ordered large quantities of a special type of coffeemaker. Curiosity got the best of him; in 1981 he ventured from New York City to Seattle to see what was going on at this little company called Starbucks Coffee, Tea and Spice. Here he saw what the company owners could not see, and he wanted to be a part of what he envisioned as a tremendous opportunity. Through persistence, Schultz finally convinced the owners in 1982 to hire him.

After he became director of marketing and operations, he took a trip to Italy, which led to another vision. Schultz noticed that coffee bars existed on nearly every street corner in the cities of Italy. They not only served excellent espresso, they were also gathering places where Italians connected socially. By his calculations, there were nearly two hundred thousand such coffee bars throughout the country.

Unfortunately, the owners of Starbucks could not see the vision Schultz so clearly saw. So, he quit and began his own coffee-bar business with $400,000 in seed capital. By 1986 Schultz had $1.25 million in equity. The following year, he purchased the original Starbucks company for $3.8 million, and by 1992, Schultz's Starbucks had opened 150 stores.

Schultz's traditional values led him to build a company with "soul." He had seen his father work hard, but always at low-paying jobs. As a consequence, Schultz built into his company strong value-based practices never accorded to his father. For example, Schultz insisted that all employees working twenty hours a week minimum would receive comprehensive health coverage. He also introduced an employee stock-option plan. The work environment and policies at Starbucks result in strong employee loyalty and very low worker turnover despite the company's relatively low salaries.

Today you will find Starbucks in more than twenty-five countries, serving millions of people a week. The company is expanding through new outlets so fast that its growth is difficult to keep up with. And that's just the beginning. Schultz considers Starbucks to be in its infancy. "We have less than 6 percent market share of coffee consumption," Schultz says.

In addition to vision, strategy, a strong work ethic, and the belief that a value-based culture is critical, here are the four principles Schultz considers his secrets of success:

- Don't be threatened by people smarter than you.
- Compromise anything but your core values.
- Seek to renew yourself even when you are hitting home runs.
- Remember: everything matters.

THE WALTON WONDER: SAM WALTON

Wal-Mart (NYSE: WMT) went public in 1970 at $16.50 per share. Adjusted for eleven two-for-one stock splits, the cost per share would now equal less than one penny—$0.008.

One hundred shares purchased at $16.50 would now total an astronomical 204,800 shares. At the January 2007 price of $48 per share, the initial $1,650 investment would now be worth $9,625,800. If you had invested $10,000 on the initial public offering, you would now own 1,250,000 shares, currently valued at $60,000,000.

Here's an interesting investment fact: You could have joined "Sam" years after the initial public offering and still made a fortune. A secondary offering was made twelve years later, in 1982, at an adjusted $0.20 per share. A $10,000 investment at that time would have yielded—after splits—50,000 shares, totaling a return of $2,400,000. Not bad for getting on board late.

IF YOU HAD STUDIED Sam Walton and his CEO performance strategies and invested in him when he took Wal-Mart public, you would be a very wealthy person today. To have invested in this CEO would have taken knowledge of Walton's business philosophies, the ability to monitor his decisions, and the patience and tenacity to stay the course for the long-term gain.

WALTON'S EARLY DAYS

You could say Sam Walton was born to be in retailing. His first experience came early in life when he worked in his father's store while attending school. Then, in 1940, three days after graduating from the University of Missouri, where he majored in economics, Walton went to work for JCPenney in Des Moines, Iowa. A management trainee, Walton was earning a meager $75 a month. But in early 1942, Walton resigned from JCPenney, anticipating being inducted into the military. During Walton's wait, he took a job in a DuPont munitions plant near Tulsa, Oklahoma, where he met his future wife, Helen Robson. Shortly after his wedding day, February 14, 1943, Walton began his service in the U.S. Army Intelligence Corps, supervising security at aircraft plants and prisoner of war camps.

By the time he was discharged from the military, Walton was determined to own his own department store. His dream became a reality in the fall of 1945 when he purchased a Ben Franklin five-and-dime franchise with $20,000 borrowed from his father-in-law and $5,000 saved from his military pay. His retailing leadership was evident from the onset: Walton's store led in sales and profits in the six-state region.

WALTON'S BUSINESS PHILOSOPHY

Walton had a definite philosophy: stock shelves with a wide range of goods and sell them at very low prices. In order to do this he began to experiment with discount merchandising, buying direct from the wholesaler. This enabled him to lower his price per item, a concept that allowed him to sell a greater quantity of merchandise, which in turn increased sales volume and profits. He became so successful using this concept that when his lease was up, the landlord refused to renew, wanting the business for his own son instead. Walton sold the franchise and reaped more than $50,000 in profit.

By 1950 Walton purchased a store in Bentonville, Arkansas, which he called Walton's 5 & 10. As the years passed Walton continued to expand his business, with the help of his brother, father-in-law, and brother-in-law. Eventually he decided to open much larger stores, which he called Walton's Family Centers. It was with these centers that Walton decided to offer his managers the chance to become limited partners both by investing in the store they would oversee and by investing a maximum of $1,000 in new outlets. Walton's philosophy was that if the managers were invested in the company, they would work harder to keep profits at a maximum and to improve their management skills. The concept proved successful. By 1962 Walton and his brother owned sixteen variety stores in Arkansas, Missouri, and Kansas.

WAL-MART EMERGES

The first Wal-Mart store was opened in 1962 in Rogers, Arkansas, and it didn't take long before a chain of Wal-Marts began to sprout up across much of rural America. In 1970 Sam Walton decided to take Wal-Mart public. It was during this time that he also introduced his "profit sharing plan," which enabled Wal-Mart employees to improve their income based on the profitability of the store. While this type of compensation is quite common today, Walton was among the first to implement it. According to him, it's not the individual who wins, it's the team. By giving employees an opportunity to own part of the company through stock options and store discounts, they would see that their success depended on the company's success. Thus they would focus on successful company outcomes and work more as a team.

Walton also believed that happy employees resulted in happy customers, which he believed would translate to increased sales. He was right. By the 1980s, sales from the three hundred Wal-Mart stores soared to more than $1 billion. Eleven years later Wal-Mart was recognized as the largest retailer in the United States and its stock was one of the most valued.

A Clear Vision

Throughout the years, Sam Walton never faltered from his original vision of providing the customer with the widest variety of choices at the lowest possible cost. From a business perspective he was committed to driving costs out of the merchandising system wherever they could be found—in the stores, in the manufacturer's margins of profit, and in the middleman. To stay true to his vision, Walton outlined "Ten Commandments of Business" that play an integral part in the way the company does business to this day.

1. Commit to your goals
2. Share your rewards
3. Energize your colleagues
4. Communicate all you know
5. Value your associates
6. Celebrate your success
7. Listen to everyone
8. Deliver more than you promise
9. Work smarter than others
10. Blaze your own path

Sam Walton actively managed the company—as president and CEO—until 1988, and he remained chairman of the board until his death in 1992. At that point in time the billionaire who still drove an old pickup truck was recognized as the world's second richest man. Walton believed his stock was "precious," and he was extremely reluctant to sell shares. As a group, his family still controls more than 39 percent of the stock, making them the wealthiest family in the world.

EASY DOES IT:
MEG WHITMAN

Pierre Omidyar was the original founder of eBay and continues to own 15 percent of the company. Yet, similar to many successful entrepreneurs, he had the foresight to enlist a top-quality CEO—in this case, Margaret (Meg) Whitman—to run the business. Under their leadership eBay became one of the few really big hits based on Internet trading.

eBay has only been public since September 1998 (NAS-DAQ: EBAY). Adjusted for stock splits, the opening cost would have been $0.75 per share. An initial investment of $10,000 would currently be 13,334 shares; at the current price of $32 per share, they would be worth $427,000. In fewer than eight years, you would have made forty-two times your money.

IN THE FALL OF 2004 *Fortune* magazine wrote that Meg Whitman was the "most powerful woman in American Business." In seven years as CEO and president of eBay, she led that company's growth from $5.7 million to $3.2 billion—the fastest growth of any company in history. Yet, Whitman says, it's eBay's customers who built the business. That's her unassuming approach to leadership. It's also been her leadership style to be counterintuitive about strategic decisions. For example, during her first few years at eBay, when other Internet companies were jumping into advertising, Whitman focused instead on the consumer market and collectibles, the things she thought the most passionate users cared about. Then in 2002, long after other Internet companies had squandered money on huge advertising ventures, Whitman cautiously ventured into the game.

While Whitman may be talented at knowing when to do nothing, don't think she's totally reluctant to take risks. She's actually taken some pretty bold bets. Over the objections of some of her top executives, she bought PayPal rather than develop eBay's own payment system. The acquisition is said to have been a great one for eBay.

In a similar fashion, Whitman has made big bets with personnel. In 1999, when eBay's website crashed for twenty-two hours and the young company risked losing its entire base of customers and transaction data, Whitman recognized a "glaring weakness" in their in-house talent to fix the site. But she didn't blame them; she blamed herself for not "going with her gut" early on when she had suspicions that the site had not been built sturdily enough to handle incredible growth volumes. To correct the problem she pleaded with Gateway's tech boss to come to eBay and opted to pay him an annual salary of $450,000 and 500,000 options at a time when she herself was earning merely $195,000 and 100,000 options. Consequently, in any given day, the infrastructure that Maynard G. Webb built can handle more transactions than NASDAQ. In nearly four years there have been no outages.

Whitman grew up on Long Island and attended Princeton, where she majored in economics, and later Harvard Business School. She learned all about brand management at Procter & Gamble and picked up strategy at Bain & Company. When she moved to Disney she learned all about strategy before leaving to follow her neurosurgeon husband to the East Coast. She later worked at Stride Rite, FTD, and Hasbro. Her consumer marketing background made her an attractive candidate for eBay's CEO in 1998. Her folksy, approachable style also seemed to fit what the eBay community would like. Even today, that genuine friendliness prevails. At an "eBay Live" event for users, Whitman was seen autographing T-shirts and casually visiting with the throngs of attendees.

With the success of initial growth, Whitman has taken eBay global, hoping to increase overseas revenues from 10 percent to 50 percent in a two-year period. All the while, she will continue to create one of the largest operating margins of all publicly traded dot.coms—a noteworthy 30 percent.

CONCLUSION

IN *FINDING MIDAS* we have discussed a simple method that can produce mega-stock gains.

As with the use of any tool, however, if you do not use it correctly, results will not accrue. We have discussed the need for having a diversified portfolio, with upwards of at least ten positions. We have emphasized the need to think long term and to be patient. Most important is to let profits run and to sell those positions that are not meeting the criteria. We have discussed when to sell.

We have presented a number of case studies showing the possible results from this method of investing. We have discussed how we use the Entrepreneurial CEO Investing method at RENN Capital Group, Inc. and our results.

Ours is a simple system. Remember these four main criteria:

1. CEO and management have a major stake in the business, that is, "skin in the game"

2. A clear vision with above-average growth prospects
3. Profitable operations now
4. A reasonable valuation when you select the position

To learn more about the CEO mega-stock method, contact us at www.ceoinvesting.net. Best wishes in your investment portfolio, and *have fun* doing it.

The following chart shows the results from investing in ten companies. It shows when the company became publicly traded and the number of shares you would have today after stock splits. It does not show cash dividends paid, which would make returns even higher. We used $100,000 to illustrate the returns you would have made. The chart shows the numbers of years being publicly traded. Following the chart is a schedule of compound return results so you can also see the returns over years.

THE COMPOUND ANNUAL GROWTH RATE

Company	Year	Compound Annual Growth
Berkshire Hathaway	42	23.3%
Dell	19	37.1%
Microsoft	21	35.3%
AutoZone	16	22.4%
Southwest Airlines	36	15.6%
Clear Channel Communications	26	21.0%
Countrywide Financial	38	16.7%
Starbucks	15	28.5%
Wal-Mart	37	27.3%
eBay	9	59.9%

CEO	Company & Symbol	Year Co. Went Public	Years Since Public	Adjusted Price	Shares	Current Price	$10,000 Investment	$100,000 Investment
Warren Buffett	Berkshire Hathaway (BRK/A)*	1965	42	$20.00	500	$108,850.00	$54,425,000	$544,250,000
Michael Dell	Dell (DELL)	1988	19	$0.09	111,111	$26.25	$2,917,000	$29,170,000
Bill Gates	Microsoft (MSFT)	1986	21	$0.07	142,857	$29.80	$4,257,000	$42,570,000
J. R. Hyde III	AutoZone (AZO)	1991	16	$5.75	1,729	$119.60	$207,000	$2,070,000
Herb Kelleher	Southwest Airlines (LUV)	1971	36	$0.10	100,000	$16.00	$1,600,000	$16,000,000
Lowry Mays	Clear Channel Communications (CCU)	1981	26	$0.32	31,250	$37.60	$1,175,000	$11,175,000
Angelo Mozilo	Countrywide Financial Corp. (CFC)	1969	38	$0.14	71,428	$42.00	$3,000,000	$30,000,000
Howard Schultz	Starbucks (SBUX)	1992	15	$1.06	9,434	$35.50	$335,000	$3,350,000
Sam Walton	Wal-Mart (WMT)	1970	37	$0.008	1,250,000	$48.00	$60,000,000	$600,000,000
Meg Whitman	e-Bay (EBAY)	1998	9	$0.75	13,334	$32.00	$427,000	$4,270,000

* Represents Berkshire Hathaway the year Warren Buffett took over as CEO (All "current" prices are based on the date January 4, 2007.)

When you look at the numbers from an annual compound basis, one observation comes to mind: while the absolute returns are phenomenal, the compound return per year seems within reason. For example, $10,000 investment in Wal-Mart since becoming public resulted in $59,750,000 value as of January 2007 (see table on page 136). The compound annual return was 27.3 percent. In looking at the numbers you will quickly see that any annual rate above 15 percent results in huge gains over time.

You will also see that the longer the period, the lower the compound annual return. For example, Dell, Microsoft, and eBay have been publicly trading less than companies such as Wal-Mart and Berkshire Hathaway. These companies have rates above 30 percent; eBay is a whopping 59.9 percent after being public a mere eight years.

ABOUT THE AUTHORS

Russell Cleveland, CFA

Russell Cleveland is the principal founder and the majority share-holder of RENN Capital Group, Inc., which provides capital to emerging publicly owned companies. Cleveland is a Chartered Financial Analyst who has specialized in investing in emerging growth companies for more than 40 years. He is a graduate of the University of Pennsylvania's Wharton School.

Cleveland has served as president of the Dallas Association of Investment Analysts. Prior to founding his own firm he held executive positions with major southwest regional brokerage firms. For more than ten years he was a contributing editor of *Texas Business* magazine, where he analyzed investment trends. He is the coauthor of *Money Grows in Texas* and the SMI course "Being Financially Independent." He has been quoted in numerous national and international financial publications, including the *Wall Street Journal*, *Barron's*, *Equities* magazine, *Business Week*, *Financial Times*, *Investment Week*, *International Investment*, *Fund Strategy*, and *Professional Advisor*. Cleveland has also appeared on CNBC-TV as a commentator reviewing small-cap companies.

Cleveland currently serves as president and director of Renaissance Capital Growth & Income Fund III, Inc. (NASDAQ: RENN). He is also director and manager of Renaissance U.S. Growth and Income Trust PLC, which is traded on the London Exchange, and is U.S. portfolio manager of U.S. Special Opportunities Trust, PLC (based in London), and investment manager for a new British open-end fund, Premier RENN. He currently serves on the board of directors of Cover-All Technologies, Inc.; CaminoSoft Corp.; Integrated Security Systems, Inc.; Access Plans USA; RUSGIT; and Tutogen Medical, Inc. Through the years Cleveland has served on the boards of many publicly traded emerging growth companies.

On a personal note, Cleveland is married and has three grown sons. He has a long history of interest in music and helped create the definitive book on classical guitars, *The Classical Guitar: A Complete History*, featuring the Russell Cleveland guitar collection. He is a descendent of Moses Cleveland, who arrived in America in 1640, and was the forefather of many prominent Americans, including President Grover Cleveland.

BETTE PRICE, CMC

Bette Price is an international author, consultant, and award-winning print and broadcast journalist who, since 1982, has been president and CEO of The Price Group, a Dallas-based consulting firm dedicated to assessing and developing leadership, planning, and performance issues. She is certified in the science of how and why people perform and has earned the certified management consultant designation from the Institute of Management Consultants, USA.

Price is the author of *True Leaders*, and her articles on leadership, values, and ethics are published extensively in numerous trade publications. She is a recognized expert in ethical leadership issues and is a frequent source to the media, having been quoted in such publications as the *Wall Street Journal*, *USA Today*, the *Oregonian*, the *Chicago Tribune*, *Harvard Management Update*, *Insight Magazine*, Tribune Media Services, Knight-Ridder newspapers, *Investors Business Daily*, and the *Dallas Morning News*.

Price's clients range from small- to mid-size entrepreneurial companies to such major corporations as IBM, Prudential Asset Resources, Sony Electronics, Washington Mutual, and Smurfit-Stone Waste Reduction Services. She is a member of the Institute of Management Consultants, USA; the National Speakers Association; and the National Association of Women Business Owners. She is also a fellow of the distinguished Legacy Center for Public Policy.

PORTFOLIO NOTES

PORTFOLIO NOTES